RECIPES FOR HEALTH

Gluten-Free

By the same author:
Diets to Help Multiple Sclerosis
Diets to Help Coeliacs
Recipes for Health: Wheat, Milk & Egg-Free

RECIPES FOR HEALTH

Gluten-Free

Over 100 recipes for those allergic to gluten

RITA GREER

Thorsons
An Imprint of HarperCollins*Publishers*

Thorsons
An Imprint of HarperCollins*Publishers*
77–85 Fulham Palace Road,
Hammersmith, London W6 8JB
1160 Battery Street,
San Francisco, California 94111–1213

First published 1978 as *Gluten Free Cooking*
Second edition, revised,
enlarged and reset, 1983
Third edition 1989
This edition revised
and updated 1995

3 5 7 9 10 8 6 4 2

© Rita Greer, 1995

Rita Greer asserts the moral right to
be identified as the author of this work

A catalogue record for this book
is available from the British Library

ISBN 0 7225 3198 2

Typeset by
Harper Phototypesetters Limited, Northampton, England
Printed and bound in Great Britain by
Caledonian International Book Manufacturing Ltd,
Glasgow

Contents

1

Cooking for a Gluten-Free Diet

THE SUDDEN introduction of a special diet into the running of a household can be a traumatic experience. Often there is very little help available at the crucial beginning of the diet, especially if there is no dietitian to give advice. If the situation is badly handled the special dieter can unintentionally be made to feel abnormal and a nuisance. A child on a strict diet can instinctively feel he or she is a source of worry as the mealtime routine is suddenly changed.

My advice is don't get into a panic and don't despair. Instead, direct your energy into getting reorganized in the kitchen in order to cope with the new and challenging situation on your domestic front. Hundreds of thousands of people all over the world are in your predicament, so don't feel you are alone and that the problem is gigantic. It isn't anything that cannot be sorted out easily.

SOME QUESTIONS ANSWERED

What Exactly is Gluten?

If you take a teaspoonful of wheat flour and mix it with a little water the result will be an elastic sort of paste, firmly bound together. The ingredient that makes it bind like this is the *gluten* in the wheat – the 'elastic'. The gluten is actually protein and in a normal diet is a valuable addition. A similar effect is obtained when mixing rye, barley or oat flour with water. Items such as bread can have extra gluten added, as in the so-called 'strong' flours. However, it does not hurt anyone to live without it and millions of people all over the world go the whole of their lives without ever having eaten it, with no ill effects.

Where is Gluten Found?

It is found mainly in wheat, but also in rye, barley and oats. It is only found in *grains* and the diagram below shows what they look like before they are ground into flour. *Note:* There is no gluten in rice although it is an important grain product.

What are Wheat, Rye, Barley and Oats Used for?

These are mainly used for making bread, cakes, biscuits, pastry and breakfast cereals. Wheat is the most widely used of the four. They are also added to products to thicken them and make them smooth and to help bind them together. For example they can be put into the sauce that goes with baked beans and into instant puddings.

The flour you buy in the shops for baking is wheat flour, whether plain or self-raising, and the same flour is used in commercial baking for shop bread, cakes, pastries, buns, biscuits etc. Wheat flour is mixed with other grains to give a base for special breads such as rye bread.

Are Any Gluten-free Items Readily Available?

Yes, lots! All fruit and vegetables, meat, fish, pulses, eggs, cheese, milk, butter, cooking oils and nuts are gluten-free.

Is Gluten-free Cooking More Difficult than Ordinary Cooking?

Old fashioned gluten-free cooking was difficult and dull, but the recipes in this book will show you that in most cases it is easier and more delicious than ordinary cooking.

Because manufacturers are not geared to the gluten-free dieter's needs, their labelling can quite inadvertently lead to confusion. If a product lists any of the following substances on the label it may contain gluten, so do check carefully. A good maxim is when in doubt leave it out of your diet.

flour	special edible starch
modified starch	food starch
corn	starch
cornstarch	thickener
rusk	thickening
cereal	binding
cereal protein	binder
edible starch	vegetable protein

How Can You Tell Which Commercial Products Contain Gluten?

The following ingredients always contain flour from wheat, rye, barley or oats and therefore are not gluten free:

wheat bran	bulghar/bulgar wheat
wheat flour	granary flour
wheat berries	rye meal
wheatmeal	rye flour
wheat flakes	rye flakes
wheat protein	barley meal
wheat starch (sometimes	barley flakes
described as special gluten-	barley flour
free starch, although it is	pearl barley
not 100 per cent gluten free)	pot barley

wholewheat	oats
cracked wheat	porridge oats
kibbled wheat	rolled oats
durum wheat	jumbo oats
semolina	oat flakes
couscous	oatbran
wheatgerm	oatgerm
pourgouri	oatmeal
burghul	pinhead oatmeal

'Starch' can mean anything from wheat flour to potato flour. 'Cornflour' can also cover a multitude of sins and can mean all sorts of starches mixed up (UK).

You will find instructions on how to approach manufacturers for information on page 8.

Here is a list of common products likely to contain gluten. Although it is a long list, don't worry! Most of it is 'junk' food and is best avoided in any case.

baby foods	malt
baked beans	mayonnaise
baking powder	meat with stuffing/coatings
batter and pancake mixes	muesli
bedtime drinks	mustard
biscuits and biscuit mixes	pancakes, pancake mixes
blancmange	pastas
breakfast cereals	paste
burgers	pastry, pastry mixes
cakes, cake mixes	pepper (white, catering)
cherries (glacé/candied)	pickles

chocolates

chutney

cocoa, drinking chocolate

coffee (cheap brands)

communion wafers

corned beef

cornflour (cornstarch)

chopped peel

cream (non-dairy)

crispbreads

crisps

crumble topping

curry powder

custard powder

custard (ready made)

desserts/instant puddings

fish in crumbs, batter or
    coatings

gravy powder/mixes

ice cream

macaroni

pie fillings

porridge

potato, instant

puddings

salad dressings

sandwich spreads

sauces

sausages

snacks

soups (tinned/packet)

soy sauce

spaghetti

spreads

sprouted grains

stock powder/paste

stuffing

suet

sweets

yoghurts

For a list of gluten-free products see pages 153–4.

Gluten-free?

Legally, manufacturers can label food 'gluten-free' even if it contains a little gluten (UK). This depressing state of affairs is due to an old ruling by the World Health Organization (WHO). Other countries, such as Germany and France, have a more honest 100 per cent gluten-free standard. The ingredient at the centre of the scandal is wheat starch. This is wheat from which most – but not all – gluten has been processed out with most of its other nutrients. Because it is a waste product it is cheap, and it is the most widely used flour for commercial gluten-free baking. The majority of people who eat it have no idea that it is not truly gluten free and nor do the people who prescribe it for gluten-free diets.

Rest assured, all the recipes in this book are at the higher 100 per cent gluten-free standard and wheat starch is not used at all.

Are There Any Types of Flour which are Naturally Gluten-Free?

Yes, there are four major ones: ground rice, corn/maize flour (cornmeal/cornstarch), potato flour and soya flour. All these are used in the recipes in this book.

Is There Any Way You Can Find out which Products Contain Gluten?

There are societies specially for people on gluten-free diets who publish lists of gluten-free foods. Unless such societies are enthusiastic, very active, and publish a new list regularly, the lists tend to be outdated and therefore misleading. Another danger is that some organizations may have favourite manufacturers and will deliberately ignore products by rival manufacturing companies, thus giving the gluten-free consumer a limited list of products that are available. By being a member of these societies such lists may (but not necessarily) be made available to you.

You can also approach manufacturers for lists. The best way is to write a straightforward letter, enclosing a stamped addressed envelope, requesting a list of their products which are gluten-free. The larger firms have these lists printed off ready for such enquiries but some firms do not reply on principle. Here is a sample letter to a firm.

Dear Sirs,

Gluten-free Products

I am cooking for a gluten-free diet and would be most grateful if you would advise me as to which of your products are gluten-free. I enclose a stamped addressed envelope.

Yours faithfully,

It is a good idea to keep a pocket notebook with your own lists of products to avoid. This will prove very helpful when out shopping.

Fan Ovens – Temperature and Baking Times

As these may vary from one model to another, only guide-lines can be given. Generally speaking, temperatures of 20° below those recommended for an ordinary oven and baking times of up to one third less should be effective.

Bear in mind that not all gluten-free foods are necessarily healthy. There are many brands of sweets, confectionery and junk foods available which happen to be gluten-free. By living just on these a health result will not be achieved. See Chapter 12 for help with balancing a gluten-free diet.

The Kitchen Cupboard

CLEAR OUT a particular corner or shelf in your kitchen for the special items you are going to need for baking and cooking. Some of the items you can make for yourself and some you can buy. All of them are suitable for the whole family so don't think it is going to be that difficult to organize.

CONTAMINATION

One of the problems of gluten-free baking is to avoid contamination by gluten-containing flours such as wheat. It can occur by contact with other items in the kitchen and store cupboard such as wheat flour; by using utensils and equipment which are also used for ordinary cooking, e.g. baking tins; and by airborne means such as flour dust from overalls and aprons. Other dangers are wheat flour under the finger-nails and wheat breadcrumbs in the toaster.

If cooking for an acutely allergic person, separate baking tins and utensils are essential. If cooking for a not-so-allergic person, ordinary tins etc. can be used if they are kept scrupulously clean.

GLUTEN-FREE ESSENTIALS FOR THE KITCHEN CUPBOARD

Cooking oil (sunflower, soya, corn, olive)

Pure almond and vanilla flavourings

Rice paper

Soy sauce (thin, gluten-free brand)

Sesame seeds

Sunflower seeds

Dried yeast, instant yeast, easy blend (check labels)

Spices (ginger, nutmeg, mixed spice – gluten-free brand – allspice, ground cloves, cinnamon etc.)

Soft, moist sugars e.g. demerara

Ground cornflour (cornstarch) rice

Potato flour

Soya flour

Wine or cider vinegar

Honey (clear)

Canned salmon, tuna, sardines in oil (not sauce)

Dried pectin (if required)

Black peppercorns

Gelatine crystals

Fruit juices (pure)

Trufree flours (all 100 per cent gluten-free)

Note

Always check food labels before classing any food as gluten-free.

Emergency Gluten-Free Menus

Just to give you a practical helping hand to start, here are some emergency menus that can easily be followed until you have found sources of the few special ingredients and products you will need for a new and interesting diet.

ADULTS

Eat only the foods specified. They are easily obtainable and most will already be in the store cupboard or refrigerator. Use sea salt and freshly ground black pepper for seasoning. Put polyunsaturated margarine or butter on hot vegetables. Drink tea or coffee with milk. Wine, port, sherry and brandies may be drunk, but no other types of alcohol.

Breakfast

Rice Krispies or *Cornflakes* (UK), milk and sugar; grilled bacon, poached or fried egg, grilled tomatoes, fried mushrooms; pure fruit juice. Don't be tempted to eat bread or any other breakfast cereals. If *Rice Krispies* or *Cornflakes* are unobtainable, make a muesli-type cereal yourself from 1 to 2 heaped tablespoonsful of cold cooked brown rice (boiled the previous day), a sprinkling each of raisins, sesame and sunflower seeds, an eating apple (grated), a little liquid honey to sweeten and milk or fruit juice to moisten.

Midday Meal

Boiled or baked potatoes; fresh salad of tomatoes, lettuce, cucumber, grated carrot; tinned salmon, tuna or sardines in oil or water. Make a dressing from 2 teaspoonsful sunflower oil (or similar), a squeeze of fresh lemon juice, a pinch or two of raw cane sugar, sea salt and freshly ground black pepper. If you wish to eat a dessert of some kind, choose any type of fresh fruit – bananas, grapes, apples, oranges, pears etc.

Dinner

Grilled lamb chop or small steak; 2 plain boiled or steamed green vegetables – cabbage, French (snap) beans, peas, sprouts etc; plain brown rice, boiled. If you feel the need for a gravy, save the meat juices from the grill pan, strain them off, discard the fat and pour in some of the water strained from the vegetables. Mix well with a wooden spoon and add half a ripe tomato, mashed. Season to taste. Do not use any kind of gravy mix.

Snacks

Allow yourself up to 3 bananas per day, a few plain almonds or walnuts (English walnuts) and dried fruits such as apricots and raisins.

Eating out is a problem and best avoided when you start the diet. At home stick to plain, fresh ingredients and you will have no worries.

Other foods you might like to choose from are:

Cold ham (without breadcrumb coating);
Cold lamb, beef or pork (off a previously roasted joint without stuffing);
Roast beef or lamb or pork with roast potatoes;
Boiled root vegetables such as carrots, parsnips, turnips.

Without bread, cakes and biscuits (cookies) your starch intake will be too low. Eat plenty of potatoes and rice to make up for this.

Bear in mind that these are emergency menus and are a little narrow in outlook for a long-term gluten-free diet. However, with this information you should be able to get started immediately rather than continue with an ordinary diet until you have reorganized your eating regime in a broader way. No matter how tempting, *do not eat ordinary bread, cakes and biscuits* etc.

Here is a shopping list/storecupboard check for emergency menus:

Cornflakes or *Rice Krispies* (if available)	Cooking oil (sunflower or olive)
Milk	Almonds and walnuts
Sugar	(English walnuts)
Bacon	sardines – all canned in oil
Eggs	or water (not sauce)

Pure fruit juice
Sesame and sunflower
seeds
Fresh meat or fish (plain)
Fresh fruit
Dried fruit
Fresh vegetables
Tomato *Purée* (paste)

Salmon, tuna (tunny),
Sea salt
Black peppercorns
Brown rice (plain)
Butter or margarine
Tea or coffee (plain)
Butter

EMERGENCY MENUS FOR CHILDREN

Use the emergency menus for adults but omit the alcohol
and add extra snacks such as:

Fresh orange segments sprinkled with a little raw cane
sugar;
Home-made fish cakes – (see recipe page 28);
Home-made chips – serve hot with a poached egg on top
and grilled tomatoes instead of tomato sauce (see recipe
page 82);
Savoury rice – fry a small chopped onion in a little oil.
Add chopped cooked vegetables and 1 cup (1¼ cups) of
cold cooked brown rice. Heat through while turning over
with a wooden spoon. Season and serve;
Milk shakes – blend 2 cups of milk with any piece of
stoned, peeled fruit. Add sugar to taste and blend. (You
will need a blender/liquidizer for this.)

4

Staple Substitutes

There is one very important food around which a gluten-free diet revolves. This is bread, and life without it can be difficult; there is no way to fill the gap left by wheat bread other than to substitute another kind that is just as nutritious and versatile. Here are five recipes for gluten-free bread which are easy to make and comfortably fill this gap. (They are also easy to make.) Unfortunately, they are expensive compared with ordinary bread.

ACTIVE DRIED YEAST

This is not mixed into the flour like Easyblend (instant) yeast. It needs to be mixed with warm water and allowed to swell before adding to the flour. If you are using this type of yeast, take some of the water from the recipe, warm it and sprinkle in the yeast with the sugar. Leave it in a warm place until frothy, then stir and add to the flour with the rest of the liquid. Please note that brewer's yeast is not suitable for baking.

'PLAIN' LOAF

This loaf has an attractive golden crust and a creamy coloured centre. Al the ingredients are naturally pale in colour (i.e. they are not bleached or processed to make them pale). The flour blend used comprises naturally gluten-free flours based on wholefood principles. The brown specks in the flour are caused by the brown skins on the wholeground almonds which are part of the blend.

Metric/Imperial		American
290g/10¼oz	*Trufree* No. 4 flour	2½ cups
1 tbs	sunflower oil	1 tbs
1 sachet	yeast (provided with	1 sachet
or	the flour)	or
7g/¼oz	instant yeast	7g/¼oz
Exactly	warm water	1 cup
225ml/8fl oz		

1. Preheat oven to 350°F/180°C/gas mark 4.
2. Put the flour in a bowl, add the oil and sprinkle in the yeast.
3. Stir well, pour in the water and mix to a creamy batter.
4. Spoon into a greased 1 lb (½ kilo) loaf tin and place immediately on the top shelf of the oven to bake.
5. When golden brown, well risen and crusty (after about an hour), turn out of the tin and cool on a wire rack.
6. Do not cut until cold. Store in a clean, sealed polythene bag.

This bread does not have to be kneaded or proved (left to rise). It takes only a minute to prepare and can be sliced thinly, toasted or fried. This recipe will only work with *Trufree* No. 4 or No. 5 flours. The size of the tin is important – it should be 15x9x7cm/6x3½x2¾ in.

CRUSTY BROWN BREAD

Make and bake exactly as for Crusty 'Plain' Bread but use *Trufree* No. 5 flour which is brown.

Note to Cooks

If you cannot obtain *Trufree* flours, the flour blends can be made at home.

CRUSTY 'PLAIN' BREAD

Metric/Imperial		American
7g/¼ oz	Easyblend yeast	2 slightly heaped tsp
250ml/9fl oz	warm water	1 cup plus 2½ tbs
1 heaped tsp	sugar	1 heaped tbs
25g/1oz	soya flour	¼ cup
115g/5oz	potato flour (farina)	¾ cupful plus 1 tbs
25g/1oz	ground almonds	2 tbs
2 tsp	dried pectin to bind	2 tsp
2 pinches	sea salt	2 pinches
2 tsp	vegetable oil	2 tsp

1. Preheat the oven to 350°F/180°C/gas mark 4.
2. Sprinkle the yeast into the flour with the sugar. Mix well in a bowl.
3. Add the remaining ingredients. Mix, then beat to a creamy consistency, with a wooden spoon. (Do not use an electric beater as this will make the batter too tough.)
4. Grease a medium-sized loaf tin with oil and flour with maize (cornmeal) or potato flour. (Tin size should be 185x90x50mm or 7¼x3½x2¼ in.)
5. Use a wooden spoon to place the mixture in the tin and put straight in the oven on the top shelf.
6. Bake for about 1 hour until well risen, golden and crusty.

7. Turn out on to a wire rack to cool as soon as you take it out of the oven. (Do not cut until cold.)

Note to Cooks

Use this loaf as ordinary bread. Keep it stored in a clean, sealed polythene bag. This size loaf should last you 2 or 3 days. (If fresh yeast is used, allow double the amount and mix with a little of the warm water. Add 2 pinches of sugar and leave to froth before using.) Pectin must be the dried variety and not liquid. It is very expensive and acts as a binder to replace gluten.

CORNBREAD

This is a soft bread that can be served with a spoon – hence its alternative name, spoonbread – and is popular in the USA, where corn is a staple. It makes a good side dish but is not suitable for sandwiches or toast, and is best served warm from the oven. Cornmeal (not to be confused with cornflour/cornstarch) is available from health-food shops, Indian grocers and some supermarkets.

Metric/Imperial		American
1 tbs	sugar	1 tbs
¼ tsp	salt	¼ tsp
3 tsp	gluten-free baking powder	3 tsp
160g/6oz	cornmeal	1½ cups
50g/2oz	rice flour or ground rice	½ cup
1	egg	1
scant 300ml/½ pint	skimmed milk	1¼ cups
1 tbs	sunflower oil	1 tbs

1. Preheat the oven to 425°F/220°C/gas mark 7.
2. Put the sugar, salt, baking powder, cornmeal and rice flour into a bowl and stir to combine.
3. Beat the egg with the milk in a basin and stir in the oil. Add to the cornmeal mixture and stir well until you have a smooth batter.
4. Pour into a 23cm/9 in. pie dish that has been well greased with sunflower oil and bake on the top shelf of the oven for 30–35 minutes, until beginning to brown.
5. Serve straight from the oven in large spoonsful or cut into wedges.

SODA BREAD

This is the poor relation of bread made with yeast. It must be used within a few hours of baking as it does dry out. However, it is sometimes useful to be able to make a quick loaf which will bake in 20 minutes.

Metric/Imperial		American
¼ kilo/½ lb	*Trufree* No. 4 flour	2 cups
1 tsp	sugar	1 tsp
1 heaped tsp	bicarbonate of soda	1 heaped tsp
1 heaped tsp	cream of tartar	1 heaped tsp
1 tbs	vegetable oil	1 tbs
150ml/¼ pint	cold milk	⅔ cup

1. Preheat oven to 425°F/220°C/gas mark 7.
2. Put the flour into a bowl with the sugar, bicarbonate of soda (baking soda) and cream of tartar, and mix really well.
3. Spoon in the oil and rub in with the fingers.
4. Pour in the milk and mix to a stiff dough. Knead, using more of the flour, into a round loaf.
5. Put the loaf on to a greased baking sheet, cutting the top with a knife into the traditional cross. Bake for about 20 minutes.
6. Cool on a wire rack.

Variation

25g/1oz/¼ cup of dried fruit can be added to the flour to make tea-bread.

Gluten-Free

CRISPBREADS

Metric/Imperial		American
15g/½oz	rice bran	1 tbs
pinch	sea salt	pinch
90g/3½oz	*Trufree* No. 6 plain flour	½ cup less 1 tbs
25g/1oz	polyunsaturated soft margarine	2½ tbs
3 tbs	cold water	3½ tbs

1. Preheat oven to 450°F/230°C/gas mark 8.
2. Put the rice bran into a bowl with the salt and flour. Mix well.
3. Add the margarine and rub it in with the fingers until the mixture resembles fine breadcrumbs.
4. Add the cold water and mix into one lump of dough.
5. Roll out, using more flour, into a thin sheet of dough. Use a knife to cut into about 8 rectangles.
6. Use a spatula to lift them on to ungreased baking sheets and prick all over with a fork.
7. Bake for about 15 minutes and remove from baking sheets with a spatula. Leave to cool and crisp on a wire rack.
8. When cold, store in an air-tight container.

Note to Cooks

Eat these with cheese and celery as an alternative to bread. Good for picnics and lunchboxes.

BASIC STARCHY FOODS (GLUTEN-FREE)

As many starchy foods are forbidden on a gluten-free diet, such as ordinary bread, cakes, biscuits, buns, crisp-breads, pastas and pizza, etc., other starchy ingredients must take their place in order to maintain a nutritional balance. Rice, potatoes and bananas are all easily available, high in starch and, mercifully, gluten-free. Other such ingredients are tapioca, sago, millet, buckwheat (saracen corn) and kasha, the toasted form of buckwheat. This commodity is gluten free in spite of its name, and is a member of the same botanical family as rhubarb and sorrel.

Potatoes

Potatoes can be cooked in a huge variety of ways and there are always several types on sale all year round, which makes a gluten-free diet more interesting.

Boiled If the potatoes are new, cook them in their skins in boiling, salted water for 20–25 minutes, depending on size, until tender. Old potatoes should be peeled and cut into evenly sized pieces first, then cooked for up to 30 minutes, depending on variety.

Mashed Boil old, floury varieties such as King Edwards and Cara until tender, then drain. Mash them in the saucepan with a knob of butter, a little milk and a pinch or two of freshly grated nutmeg, salt and freshly ground black pepper. They can be kept warm for a while in the oven.

Baked (Jacket Potatoes) Scrub old potatoes really well, cutting out any eyes or blemishes. Prick all over with a fork and bake for an hour in an oven preheated to 425°F/220°C/gas mark 7 or for 2 hours at 180°C/350°F/gas mark 4. Cut open and insert a knob of butter to serve. Leftover baked potatoes can be sliced, including skin, and fried in a little sunflower or olive oil the following day.

Roast Potatoes Peel old potatoes and cut them into even-sized chunks. Place in a roasting tin and sprinkle with 1 teaspoon sunflower or olive oil for each medium-sized potato. Turn over by hand to coat the potato chunks with the oil, then roast at the top of the oven for about an hour on a high heat or 1½ hours on a medium heat until crisp, golden and tender.

Chips (French Fries) Many brands of oven chips are not gluten-free, so it is safer to make your own (see page 82).

Potato Spaghetti A useful, quick way to cook potatoes, especially for breakfast as they only take 10 minutes. See recipe on page 96.

Potato Patties Peel old potatoes, then boil and mash them. Season to taste. Form into small balls, then flatten and shallow fry in a little hot olive oil or sunflower oil until crisp and golden.

Potato Flour (farina), available from health-food shops, is useful for coating foods before frying and for thickening gravies, stews, casseroles and sauces.

Rice

Rice is widely available and there are many varieties. Serve basmati rice with curries and use other varieties for puddings and savoury dishes. Boil in plenty of water. The cooking time depends on the hardness of the grains, and varies from 10–15 minutes for basmati to 45 minutes for brown rice. When the rice is tender, drain through a colander and serve. Keep it hot, if necessary, by placing the colander over a pan of simmering water, covering with a saucepan lid or plate and just leaving until required. To reheat rice, put it into a metal sieve over a pan of water and bring to the boil. Steam for a few minutes, until hot.

Ground and flaked rice are good additions to the kitchen cupboard for a gluten-free diet. Rice flour is more finely ground than ground rice but is not easy to come by. Flaked rice is used for puddings.

Buckwheat (saracen corn) is not from the wheat family and does not contain gluten. It is cooked in the same way as rice. Kasha is the toasted form of buckwheat and tastier than the plain kind. Buy from health-food shops and cook in the same way as rice. Buckwheat flour has rather limited uses but can be made into pancakes successfully.

Cornflour True cornflour (cornstarch) is finely ground maize/sweetcorn. Always check that the label specifies maize, as sometimes other grains are added that are not gluten-free.

Cornmeal This is a coarse form of ground corn on the cob (maize) and can be used to make cornbread (see recipe on page 21).

The more you can rely on cheaper staples, such as potatoes and rice, for the carbohydrates (starch) in a gluten-free diet, the cheaper the diet will be and the fewer expensive substitutes you will need. Pulses such as beans and lentils are starchy foods but many gluten-free dieters have difficulty digesting them. However, if they do not present a problem they are a good addition to the diet.

5

Breakfasts

FISH CAKES

Makes about 6

These fish cakes can be made in advance, stored in the fridge and fried as required. Do not keep for more than 36 hours before using.

Metric/Imperial		*American*
¼ kilo/½ lb	cooked fish such as haddock, cod or coley	1¼ cups
¼ kilo/½ lb	cold, boiled potato	1 cup
25g/1oz	polyunsaturated soft margarine	2½ tbs
1 heaped tbs	freshly chopped parsley	1 heaped tbs
	sea salt and freshly ground black pepper	
	Sunflower oil for frying	

1. Mash the fish with the potatoes and the margarine.
2. Add the remaining ingredients and mix well with a

fork until the fish and parsley are evenly distributed.
3. Form into round, flat cakes with the hands.
4. Fry in hot, shallow oil for 3 minutes on each side or longer if the fish cakes have been in the fridge.
5. Serve immediately with grilled tomatoes and special gluten-free bread and margarine or butter.

Variations

Tinned salmon or tuna (in water or oil) may be used instead of white fish. (Drain well before using.)

As alternatives to just plain frying, try dipping the fish cakes in beaten egg and roll them in special gluten-free breadcrumbs before frying; or brush them with milk and dip them in special gluten-free breadcrumbs.

Note to Cooks

Commercially-made fish cakes often use wheat-bread crumbs as a coating.

MUESLI

Metric/Imperial		American
1–2 tbs	suitable base – cold cooked rice	1-2½ tbs
1	ripe eating apple, washed and sliced	1
½	ripe banana (optional), sliced	½
1 tbs	raisins	1 tbs
1 tbs	chopped nuts	1 tbs
1 tsp	sesame seeds	1 tsp
1 tsp	sunflower seeds	1 tsp
	diluted fruit juice or milk	
	sugar to taste (optional)	

1. Put all the ingredients into a cereal bowl.
2. Pour over the juice or milk and serve.

Note to Cooks

Other dried fruits can be used such as chopped dried apricots or peaches, stoned prunes etc. If fresh fruit is not available, soaked dried fruit salad can be used for variation. To save time, a basic muesli of dry items can be made, stored in an air-tight jar and used as required. This way more variety can be achieved.

MUESLI BASE

Metric/Imperial		American
50g/2oz	raisins	⅓ cup
75g/3oz	chopped nuts – walnuts, cashews, Brazils, etc.	⅔ cup
50g/2oz	sesame seeds	⅓ cup
75g/3oz	sunflower seeds	¾ cup
25g/1oz	ground almonds	¼ cup
50g/2oz	chopped dried apricots	⅓ cup
50g/2oz	chopped stoned prunes	⅓ cup

1. Combine all the ingredients.
2. Store in an air-tight jar and use as required.

Note to Cooks

Use as a base with fresh fruit, sugar or liquid honey to taste and milk to moisten.

RICE PORRIDGE

This is good for cold winter mornings. Follow with grilled bacon and special gluten-free bread fried on one side in hot vegetable oil.

Metric/Imperial		American
¼ litre/½ pint	milk	1⅓ cups
2 tbs	ground brown rice	2½ tbs
2 tsp	vegetable oil	2 tsp
1 tbs	sultanas/golden seedless raisins or chopped dried apricots	1 tbs
2 heaped tsp	sugar	2 heaped tsp
15g/½oz	ground almonds	2½ tbs

1. Put the milk and ground rice into a saucapan and stir until smooth.
2. Add the oil and dried fruit and heat to boiling point. Cook while stirring with a wooden spoon for a few minutes until the porridge thickens and the fruit swells.
3. Add the sugar and almonds. Stir well and serve hot.

POTATO AND BEANS

Metric/Imperial		American
	vegetable oil for frying	
2	baked or boiled potatoes, cut into slices	2
1 portion	gluten-free baked beans in tomato sauce	1 portion

1. Put a little oil in the frying pan and heat. Add the potato slices and cook on both sides until golden and crisp.
2. At the same time, heat the beans in a small saucepan.
3. Serve at once on a warmed plate.

Note to Cooks

The potatoes can be cooked the day before, either baked in their skins or boiled in salted water. Use a gluten-free brand of baked beans such as Heinz. Check the label before using.

BEANS ON TOAST

Toast thick slices gluten-free bread. Spread with poly-unsaturated soft margarine and top with hot gluten-free baked beans in tomato sauce.

BUBBLE AND SQUEAK

Fry leftover greens and potato (pre-cooked and chopped up) in the frying pan with a little vegetable oil to prevent it sticking. Trun over and fry on the other side. Season with sea salt and freshly ground black pepper. Serve hot with grilled bacon.

KEDGEREE

Although this sounds a rather strange dish for breakfast, it was a popular item on the menu for the Victorian breakfast table as it made use of the leftovers of the previous day. It could certainly be made the night before and reheated for breakfast.

Metric/Imperial		American
2–3 heaped tbs	cooked brown rice	2½-3½ heaped tbs
50g/2oz	cooked, flaked haddock or cod	⅓ cup
1	medium-sized tomato, chopped small	1
1	egg, hard-boiled	1
	sea salt and freshly ground black pepper	
	vegetable oil	

1. Mix together the first three ingredients and season.
2. Heat a little oil in a saucepan. Add the rice mixture and heat through while stirring gently. Top with chopped hard-boiled egg.
3. Season and serve hot on a warmed plate.

BREAKFAST PLATTER

Metric/Imperial		American
50g/2oz	lamb's liver or kidneys	1 small piece
	gluten-free cornflour	
2 slices	back bacon	2 slices
2 slices	special gluten-free bread	2 slices
2	medium-sized tomatoes	2

1. Wash the liver or kidneys and cut out any strings etc., then cut it into slices.
2. Dip the slices in flour (cornstarch) and fry in a little hot vegetable oil.
3. At the same time, put the bacon, bread and tomatoes under a hot grill, turning the bread over to toast both sides.
4. Serve on a warmed plate with the tomatoes on the toast.

Variation: Fry 3 or 4 sliced mushrooms with the liver.

LEMON PANCAKES

Makes 3

Metric/Imperial		American
50g/2oz	*Trufree* No. 7 S.R. flour	¼ cup
1	egg	1
150ml/¼ pint	milk or milk and water	⅔ cup
pinch	sea salt	pinch
	vegetable oil for frying	
	sugar	
	fresh lemon juice	

1. Put the flour and egg into a basin and mix to a stiff paste – don't worry about the lumps at this stage.
2. Gradually add the milk and beat out the lumps.
3. Sprinkle in the salt.
4. Heat the frying pan and pour in a little oil. Add one third of the batter, tilting the pan so that the base is covered.
5. Cook for about 2 minutes then turn it over with a spatula and cook on the other side.
6. Serve immediately, sprinkled with sugar and lemon juice. Roll up or stack to serve.

OTHER BREAKFAST SUGGESTIONS

Cheese on Toast

Toast slices of special gluten-free bread on both sides. Cover one side with thin slices (or grated) Cheddar cheese. Grill for a minute. Put slices of tomato on the cheese and continue grilling until the cheese is bubbly and the tomato cooked.

Bacon and Egg

Grill slices of back bacon. Serve with a poached egg on special gluten-free toast.

Cowboy's Breakfast

Serve slices of grilled bacon with hot gluten-free baked beans in tomato sauce on special gluten-free bread.

Scrambled Egg

Serve 2 eggs scrambled with a little milk on special gluten-free toast. Garnish with grilled tomatoes or fried mushrooms.

Boiled Egg and Toast Fingers

Lightly boil an egg (3 or 4 minutes). Serve with fingers of buttered special gluten-free toast.

Omelette filled with Fried Mushrooms

Make an omelette with 2 eggs. Fill with 50g/1oz mushrooms, fried in a little sunflower oil or similar.

Note to Cooks

To top up any of these, serve a gluten-free cereal, milk and brown sugar or special gluten-free toast, butter and marmalade.

6

Snacks

Snacks may be an important feature of a diet for those who experience a sudden weight loss when they change over from an ordinary diet to a gluten-free one. As all fruit (fresh) is gluten-free, what could be more simple than a piece of fruit as a snack? Bananas are particularly useful and should be regarded as a staple food.

The following recipes are for both sweet and savoury snacks. Biscuits and cookies can be baked in batches and stored in air-tight containers to be used as required. Don't make the mistake of storing biscuits and cookies together as the cookies, being moist, will soften the biscuits. Any biscuits which do go soft in storage can easily be recrisped in the oven for a few minutes.

SANDWICHES

As most commercial spreads contain gluten you will need to fall back on home-made spreads and sandwich fillings. One consolation about this situation is that at least you will know exactly what you are eating!

Use special gluten-free bread (see recipe), cut thinly and spread with margarine on one side. Spread one slice or lay on a filling and press the other slice on top. Cut off the crusts for a luxury sandwich. Open sandwiches need only the bottom slice of bread and can be decorated or garnished to look attractive. Unless very easy to manage serve these with a knife and fork.

FILLINGS/SPREADS

Always make freshly as you need them.

1. Cottage cheese and chopped dates (not too many) – this makes a very moist sandwich.
2. Hard-boiled egg, chopped and mixed with cress or watercress, finely chopped. This will give you a pale green filling which looks more interesting than most. Season with sea salt and black pepper. Best with brown special gluten-free bread (see recipe).
3. Tinned fish (in *oil*), drained and mashed with chopped hard-boiled egg and a little tomato *purée* (paste).
4. Thin slices of tomato, seasoned with sea salt and a little black pepper, sprinkled with a little raw cane sugar and a few chopped chives.

HAMBURGERS

Metric/Imperial		American
100g/4oz	lean minced beef	⅔ cup
1 thin slice	special gluten-free bread (see recipe) made into crumbs	1 thin slice
½	egg, beaten	½
	sea salt and freshly ground black pepper	
scant tsp	gluten-free soy sauce	scant tsp
½	small onion, peeled and finely chopped	½
	ground rice	
	olive oil for frying	

1. Put all the ingredients, except the last two, in a basin and mix well.
2. Shape by hand into 2 flat cakes.
3. Dip the burgers in the ground rice to give a thin coating.
4. Fry in a little hot oil, turning once, for 3 to 4 minutes on each side.
5. Serve with low-fat chips (see recipe) and grilled tomatoes.

Note to Cooks

These can be made in advance and stored in the fridge between two plates for a few hours until required. If you don't have any special gluten-free bread for crumbs, use cooked rice (chopped) or cold mashed potato.

PIZZA

Metric/Imperial		American
50g/2oz	*Trufree* No. 4 flour	½ cup
3 pinches	sea salt	3 pinches
½ tsp	cream of tartar	½ tsp
½ tsp	bicarbonate of soda	½ tsp
15g/½oz	polyunsaturated soft margarine	1 tbs
1½ tbs	cold water	1½ tbs
	vegetable oil	
	topping (from suggestions below)	

1. Preheat oven to 425°F/220°C/gas mark 7.
2. Put the first 4 ingredients into a basin and mix well.
3. Rub in the margarine and add the water.
4. Mix and knead to a soft dough, using a little more of the flour.
5. Put the dough on to a greased baking sheet and roll or press out into a flat circle.
6. Brush with oil and then arrange the chosen topping.
7. Bake on the top shelf for about 15 minutes and serve hot.

Toppings

a. Sliced tomato, grated cheese and 2 or 3 black olives;
b. Sliced tomato, sliced mushrooms and courgettes and grated cheese.
c. Sliced tomato, diced ham (without breadcrumb coating) and grated cheese.

Snacks

As most commercial biscuits are made with wheat, you will need to make your own biscuits at home.

ORANGE SHORTBREAD

Makes about 30

Metric/Imperial		*American*
75g/3oz	butter	⅓ cup
50g/2oz	soft brown (molasses) sugar	¼ cup
½	egg, beaten	½
1	small orange, finely grated rind	1
200g/7oz	*Trufree* No. 7 S. R. Flour	1 cup
2 pinches	salt	2 pinches

1. Preheat the oven to 350°F/180°C/gas mark 4.
2. Cream the butter and sugar together. Add the egg and orange rind and mix well.
3. Sprinkle in the flour and salt and mix to a stiff paste, adding a little cold water if necessary.
4. Roll out using more *Trufree* No. 7 flour on an ungreased baking (cookie) sheet. Cut into squares or other shapes with a sharp knife.
5. Prick all over with a fork and bake for about 20 minutes, until pale gold. Cool on a wire rack and then store in an airtight container.

SPICED CURRANT COOKIES

Makes 8–10

Metric/Imperial		American
50g/2oz	polyunsaturated soft margarine	¼ cup
100g/4oz	ground rice	½ cup
75g/3oz	eating apple, finely grated	1 small
40g/1½oz	raw cane sugar	¼ cup
½ tsp	gluten-free mixed spice	½ tsp
40g/1½oz	currants	¼ cup

1. Preheat oven to 450°F/230°C/gas mark 8.
2. In a bowl, blend the margarine and ground rice with a fork.
3. Add the apple, sugar, spice and currants. Knead and mix with a wooden spoon until one large ball of dough is formed.
4. Grease a baking sheet and put 8 to 10 spoonsful of the dough on to it. Spread out into cookie shapes with a knife.
5. Bake for about 20 to 25 minutes.
6. Allow the cookies to cool on a baking sheet, then remove them with a spatula and allow to cool on a wire rack. (The cookies will go crisp as they cool down.)

Note to Cooks

Eat within 48 hours of baking.

NUT BROWNIES

Metric/Imperial		American
1	egg white	1
65g/2½oz	sugar	½ cup less 1 tbs
65g/2½oz	ground nuts – almonds, hazelnuts, walnuts or mixed nuts	½ cup plus 1 tbs
1 tbs	ground brown rice	1 tbs
½	orange, grated rind of rice paper	½

1. Preheat oven to 350°F/180°C/gas mark 4.
2. Whisk the egg white until stiff.
3. Add the sugar and nuts.
4. Stir in the ground rice and orange rind.
5. Roll into rounds and place on a baking sheet lined with rice paper, with plenty of space between them.
6. Bake on the centre shelf for 20 to 25 minutes.
7. Allow to grow almost cold and then take them off the baking sheet.
8. Trim off the surplus rice paper with kitchen scissors.

APRICOT AND CINNAMON COOKIES

Makes 4

Metric/Imperial		American
25g/1oz	gluten-free soft margarine	2½ tbs
50g/2oz	ground rice	½ cup
½	eating apple, finely grated	½
1 tbs	brown sugar	1 tbs
6	dried apricot halves, chopped	6
3 pinches	cinnamon	3 pinches
	sunflower oil for greasing	
2 tsp	sesame seeds	2 tsp

1. Preheat oven at 450°F/230°C/gas mark 8.
2. In a bowl, use a fork to blend the margarine and ground rice.
3. Add the apple, sugar, apricots and cinnamon. Mix with a wooden spoon until the dough forms 1 ball.
4. Grease a baking sheet with the oil. Divide the dough into 4 portions and put on the greased baking sheet, spreading each portion out with the back of a teaspoon to make a cookie shape. Sprinkle each one with ½ teaspoon sesame seeds and press them in slightly.
5. Bake above centre of oven for 20–25 minutes. Cool on the baking sheet for 2–3 minutes then lift the cookies off with a spatula. Leave to cool and grow crisp on a wire rack.
6. Eat within 24 hours of baking.

Snacks

Note to Cooks

These are robust travellers and make good food for a lunchbox or picnic.

GINGER NUTS

Metric/Imperial		American
100g/4oz	*Trufree* No. 7 S.R. flour	½ cup
1 tsp	dried ginger	1 tsp
3 pinches	powdered cloves	3 pinches
25g/1oz	polyunsaturated soft margarine	2½ tbs
50g/2oz	raw cane sugar	⅓ cup
½	egg, beaten	½
2 tbs	black treacle/molasses	2½ tbs

1. Preheat the oven to 350°F/180°C/gas mark 4.
2. Put the flour, ginger and ground cloves into a basin and mix well.
3. Beat the margarine to a light cream.
4. Add the sugar and beat again.
5. Beat in the egg and treacle.
6. Add the dry ingredients and mix to a smooth paste.
7. Knead, using more flour, and roll between the palms into about 16 balls.
8. Put on to greased baking sheets and flatten to about 50cm/2 in. in diameter.
9. Bake for 12 to 15 minutes, above centre of oven.
10. Cool on a wire rack.

PLAIN BISCUITS

Metric/Imperial		American
50g/2oz	polyunsaturated soft margarine	¼ cup
50g/2oz	raw cane sugar	⅓ cup
1	egg	1
¼ kilo/½ lb	*Trufree* No. 7 S.R. flour	1 cup

1. Preheat oven to 400°F/200°C/gas mark 6.
2. Cream the margarine and sugar.
3. Beat in the egg.
4. Add the flour and mix into one ball of dough.
5. Knead, using more of the flour, and a little cold water if too stiff.
6. Roll out the dough thinly and cut into about 20 biscuits.
7. Use a spatula to place them on ungreased baking sheets.
8. Prick the biscuits with a fork and bake on the top shelf for about 15 minutes. The biscuits should be pale gold.
9. Cool on a wire rack.

NIBBLES

Most party or cocktails titbits contain gluten so you will need to make your own. It is perhaps easier to make up little dishes with naturally gluten-free items rather than to spend ages in the kitchen baking up curious items!

Here is a list of possibles: radishes, small whole tomatoes, spring onions (scallions) – for non-sensitive tummies, celery stalks, all kinds of nuts, sunflower seeds, raisins, dried apricots and sultanas (golden seedless raisins). Remember: all fresh fruit is gluten-free.

HOT JAM SANDWICH

This is rather like a giant doughnut and looks and tastes delicious. For each sandwich you will need two slices of fairly thick bread (special), margarine, raw sugar jam (jelly) and raw cane sugar.

Heat margarine in a frying pan and fry each slice of bread on one side only, until crisp and golden. Sprinkle a little raw cane sugar on a warm plate and lay one of the slices on it, fried side down. Spread with raw sugar jam (jelly) and cover with the other slice of bread so that the fried side is uppermost. Sprinkle with a little more sugar and serve right away with a spoon.

7

Soups and Starters

Home-made soups are always far superior to the commercial ones. Serve as a snack or with a meal. Pack in a thermos for picnic meals.

Traditional soup recipes will not need any alterations to make them gluten-free. Take care with thickenings and stock. Do not add any kind of noodles unless gluten-free (special) ones. Use freshly ground black pepper instead of white pepper.

SPLIT PEA SOUP

Metric/Imperial		American
¼ kilo/½ lb	dried split peas	1 cup
1 large or 2 small	onions, peeled and sliced	1 large or 2 small
1 tbs	vegetable oil	1 tbs
½ litre/1 pint	water	2½ cups
1 tbs	thin, gluten-free soy sauce	1 tbs
¼ kilo/½ lb	carrots, trimmed, scrubbed and sliced	8 ounces
	sea salt and freshly ground black pepper	

1. Put the split peas into a fine mesh sieve and wash them under the cold tap.
2. Put the peas into a large bowl with well over ½ litre/ 1 pint of water and leave overnight to swell.
3. Fry the onion in the oil for 3 or 4 minutes. Pour in the fresh water and the soy sauce.
4. Strain the soaked peas and add them to the saucepan with the carrots and a sprinkling of salt. Bring to the boil and simmer gently with the lid on for 1 to 1¼ hours, stirring from time to time. (If the soup thickens too much, add more water.)
5. Season to taste and serve hot.

Note to Cooks

This is a very nourishing and filling soup. Serve with brown special bread or special sippets (see page 61).

WINTER VEGETABLE SOUP

Metric/Imperial		American
1	medium-sized onion, peeled and sliced	1
1 tbs	thin vegetable oil	1 tbs
1	medium-sized carrot, scrubbed and sliced thinly	1
1	small parsnip, peeled and sliced	1
1	small turnip, peeled and sliced	1
4	sprouts, trimmed and sliced	4
1	medium-sized potato, peeled and sliced	1
½ litre/1 pint	water	2½ cups
1 tbs	gluten-free soy sauce	1 tbs
	Sea salt and freshly ground black pepper	

1. Fry the onion in the oil.
2. Put in the rest of the vegetables and about half the water.
3. Bring to the boil and then simmer with the lid on for about 20 minutes.
4. Add the rest of the water to cool it down, then liquidize.
5. Return the soup to the pan and add the soy sauce and seasoning to taste.
6. Serve hot.

Gluten-Free

Variation

Just before serving, add 1 heaped tablespoonful of freshly chopped parsley.

CREAM OF MANGETOUT SOUP

Serves 2

Metric/Imperial		American
½	medium onion, chopped	½
1 tbs	sunflower oil	1 tbs
100g/4oz	mangetout (snow peas), trimmed and cut up	¼ pound
½	small potato (for thickening), sliced	½
425ml/¾ pints	water	2 cups
2–3 tsp	gluten-free soy sauce	2–3 tsp
	salt and freshly ground black pepper	
4 tsp	single (light) cream (dairy)	4 tsp

1. In a saucepan, fry the onion gently in the oil for 5 minutes or until soft; do not let it brown.
2. Add the mangetout (snowpeas), potato slices, water and soy sauce. Cover the pan and bring to the boil. Lower the heat and simmer for about 15–20 minutes.
3. Remove the pan from the heat and leave until the soup has cooled slightly. Blend in a liquidizer, then pour back into the pan and season to taste. Reheat gently, then serve with 2 teaspoons of cream swirled into each bowl of soup.

CELERY SOUP

Serves 2

Metric/Imperial		American
½	medium-sized onion, peeled and sliced	½
2 tsp	thin vegetable oil	2 tsp
2–3	stalks of celery, including leaves, washed and chopped small	2–3
150ml/¼ pint	water	⅔ cup
2 scant tsp	gluten-free soy sauce	2 scant tsp
	Sea salt and freshly ground black pepper	

1. Fry the onion in the oil until transparent.
2. Add the celery and stir-fry with the onion for 3 or 4 minutes.
3. Liquidize with the water.
4. Pour the soup back into the saucepan, bring to the boil, then simmer for 5 minutes.
5. Pour into a jug and strain back into the saucepan through a fine mesh sieve.
6. Add the soy sauce and seasoning.
7. Leave to stand for a few hours, then reheat and serve.

PARSLEY SOUP – COLD

Serves 3

Metric/Imperial		American
1	small onion, peeled and sliced thinly	1
1 tbs	vegetable oil	1 tbs
2	medium-sized potatoes, peeled and sliced thinly	2
50g/2oz	fresh parsley, washed and chopped	2 cups
3 tsp	gluten-free soy sauce	3 tsp
½ litre/1 pint	water	2½ cups
	Sea salt and freshly ground black pepper	

1. Fry the onion in the oil for 3 to 4 minutes with the lid on.
2. Add the potato slices and chopped parsley. Stir and add the soy sauce and water. Bring to the boil and simmer with the lid on for half an hour.
3. Remove from the heat and allow to cool for a few minutes. Liquidize in a blender and return to the saucepan.
4. Taste and season. Dilute with more water if you think it is too thick.
5. Allow to cool. Pour into a jug and place in the fridge for at least an hour. Serve cold from the fridge.

Gluten-Free

WATERCRESS SOUP

Serves 3

Metric/Imperial		*American*
1	medium-sized onion, peeled and sliced thinly	1
2 tsp	vegetable oil	2 tsp
1	medium-sized cold boiled potato	1
1 bunch	watercress (including stems), washed thoroughly and coarsely chopped	1 bunch
400ml/¾ pint	water	2 cups
2–3 tsp	gluten-free soy sauce	2–3 tsp
	Sea salt	

1. Fry the onion in the oil until transparent but not brown.
2. Put the onion, potato, watercress and about half the water into the liquidizer. Blend and pour into the saucepan.
3. Add the remaining water and the soy sauce. Bring to the boil and simmer for 10 minutes.
4. Season to taste and serve hot or cold.

ONION AND TOMATO SOUP

Serves 2–3

Metric/Imperial		American
2	medium-sized onions	2
25g/1oz	polyunsaturated soft margarine	2½ tbs
1	medium-sized tin tomatoes	1
1 tsp	sugar	1 tsp
2 tsp	gluten-free soy sauce	2 tsp
	Sea salt and freshly ground black pepper	

1. Fry the onion in the margarine until it is transparent.
2. Liquidize the tomatoes with the cooked onion and return to the saucepan.
3. Add the sugar, soy sauce and seasoning.
4. Bring to the boil and simmer while stirring.
5. Serve hot, diluted with water if preferred.

MUSHROOM SOUP

Serves 2

Metric/Imperial		*American*
½	medium-sized onion, peeled and sliced thinly	½
2 tsp	vegetable oil	2 tsp
50g/2oz	fresh mushrooms, washed and sliced	1 cup
¼ litre/½ pint	water	1⅓ cups
1–2 tsp	gluten-free soy sauce	1–2 tsp
	Sea salt and freshly ground black pepper	

1. Fry the onion in the oil for 3 to 4 minutes.
2. Place the fried onions, mushroom slices, water and soy sauce in a liquidizer. Blend and pour back into the saucepan.
3. Bring to the boil and simmer for about 5 minutes.
4. Season to taste and serve hot.

SIPPETS

Fry cubes of special gluten-free bread lightly in hot vegetable oil until golden. Sprinkle into hot soup and serve. (Cut the bread into thick slices and then into cubes.)

HOT GRAPEFRUIT

Serves 1

Metric/Imperial		American
½	grapefruit	½
	sugar	
	polyunsaturated soft	
	margarine	

1. Loosen the flesh of the grapefruit all round with a sharp knife, and also cut between the segments.
2. Place the grapefruit in the grill pan and sprinkle with a little sugar.
3. Put a small knob of the special margarine in the centre and grill until it begins to brown.
4. Serve immediately in a rounded bowl with a teaspoon.

LIVER PÂTÉ

Metric/Imperial		American
¼ kilo/½ lb	chicken livers	8 ounces
	Sea salt and freshly ground black pepper	
1	small onion or shallot, peeled and chopped very finely	1
1 tbs	sunflower oil	1 tbs
3 good pinches	dried mixed herbs	3 good pinches
1	small clove of garlic, peeled	1
1 tsp	sherry or white wine	1 tsp

1. Wash the livers and cut out the stringy parts and yellow pieces.
2. Dry thoroughly and chop into small pieces. Sprinkle with salt and pepper.
3. Fry the chopped onion in theoil, using a small saucepan.
4. Add the chopped liver and herbs, and crush in the garlic through a garlic press.
5. Turn up the heat a little and stir with a small wooden spoon. The liver will start to crumble and turn a pinky-brown colour. This should take about 5 minutes. Mash with a fork to a smooth paste.
6. Add the sherry or white wine. Stir, taste and correct seasoning.
7. Allow the pâté to cool, then place it in little dishes and

cover with a foil lid. Store in the fridge and eat within 3 days.

8. Serve with hot gluten-free toast or as a spread in sandwiches made with gluten-free bread (see recipes). Garnish with parsley.

Note to Cooks

Unsuitable for pregnant women.

CRUDITÉS

Served as dips with special mayonnaise (page 66), these make an ideal starter.

Radishes – scrubbed and trimmed.

Celery – scrubbed and trimmed and cut into short lengths.

Carrot – washed and trimmed and cut into matchstick shapes.

Spring Onion (Scallion) – washed and trimmed.

Cauliflower – use the crisp, white florets after washing well.

Lettuce – use just the heart leaves. Wash and pat dry with a clean tea-towel. (Any variety of lettuce will do.)

Tomato – only use if you can get small fruits. Wash and leave whole.

Fennel – cut white part into matchsticks.

Courgettes – cut into small sticks, leaving the skin on.

Red and green peppers (Bell peppers) – cut into short slices after taking out the stem and seeds.

EGG MAYONNAISE

Commercially produced mayonnaise often contains gluten. Make your own at home and enjoy a gourmet experience. Use extra virgin olive oil (cold pressed) for best results, or sunflower oil if you prefer something less robust in flavour.

Metric/Imperial		*American*
300ml/½ pint	extra virgin olive or sunflower oil	1¼ cups
1	egg	1
1	egg yolk	1
2 tbs	wine vinegar	2 tbs
½ tsp	gluten-free mustard (genuine French mustard will be suitable – look for 'made in France' on the label)	½ tsp
3 pinches	salt	3 pinches
	freshly ground black pepper	

1. Have all ingredients ready at room temperature. Measure out the oil in a jug.
2. Put the egg, egg yolk, 1 tablespoon of vinegar, mustard and salt into a liquidizer and blend for a few seconds.
3. With the motor running, slowly add the oil a few drops at a time. When about half the oil has been used you can increase the rate at which you add it.
4. Add the remaining tablespoon of vinegar and switch off. If the mayonnaise is too thick, stir in a little boiling

water (about 1 tablespoon). Do not switch on the liquidizer to incorporate it.

5. Spoon the mayonnaise into a scrupulously clean screwtop jar and label and date it. Store in the fridge and use as required but throw away any remaining after 2 weeks.

Note to Cooks

The vinegar increases the pH sufficiently to act as a deterrant for salmonella bugs. Although this should make this raw egg sauce safe it is prudent for pregnant women not to use this type of cold, uncooked sauce – just in case.

PRAWN COCKTAIL

Metric/Imperial		American
1	lettuce leaf	1
½	medium-sized tomato	½
25g/1oz	peeled prawns	2½ tbs
1 tbs	egg mayonnaise (page 66)	1 tbs
½ tsp	tomato *purée*/paste	½ tsp
4 or 5 drops	lemon juice	4 or 5 drops
3 or 4 pinches	sugar	3 or 4 pinches
	sea salt and freshly ground black pepper	
	parsley to garnish	

1. Tear the lettuce leaf into small pieces and put into a glass dish.
2. Cover with the tomato, cut into wedges.
3. Place the prawns on top.
4. Put the mayonnaise into a cup with the tomato *purée* (paste) and mix.
5. Add the lemon juice and the sugar. Stir well.
6. Taste and season with salt and pepper. Pour or spoon the dressing over the prawns. Garnish with the parsley.

MUSHROOMS À LA GRECQUE

Serves 4

Metric/Imperial		American
1	medium-sized onion, grated	1
2 tbs	sunflower oil or similar	2½ tbs
1 wineglass	dry white wine	1 wineglass
1	small clove garlic, peeled	1
350g/¾ lb	button mushrooms	6 cups
4	medium-sized fresh tomatoes	4
	Sea salt and freshly ground black pepper	
	freshly chopped parsley	

1. Fry the onion in the oil, but do not let it brown.
2. Add the wine and crush in the garlic through a garlic press.
3. Wash the mushrooms and leave them whole.
4. Stab each tomato with a fork and plunge into boiling water. As they split, remove and peel them. Cut into quarters.
5. Put the mushrooms and tomato quarters into the onion mixture. Cook for about 10 minutes until the liquid has halved in quantity.
6. Season to taste and leave to grow cold. Chill in the fridge and serve in small dishes with a sprinkling of parsley. At the same time, serve fingers of special gluten-free toast and margarine or butter.

Variation

If you do not want to make this with white wine, use a non-fizzy kind of apple juice instead.

SUGGESTIONS FOR OTHER STARTERS

Melon.

Fresh grapefruit with a little sugar.

Mixed grapefruit and orange segments with a little sugar.

Avocado with prawns and egg mayonnaise (page 66).

Radishes or tomatoes with special gluten-free bread and butter.

Green salad of lettuce (2 kinds), watercress, cucumber, green pepper strips etc. Sprinkle with 3 pinches of sugar, sea salt and freshly ground black pepper, 2 teaspoonful of olive oil and 1 teaspoonful of wine vinegar. Serve in individual bowls.

8

Main Meals

EGG FLORENTINE

Serves 1

Metric/Imperial		*American*
100g/4oz	cooked and well drained spinach, chopped small	½ cup
15g/½oz	butter	1 tbs
	grated nutmeg	
	sea salt and freshly ground black pepper	
1	egg	1
1 tbs	Parmesan cheese	1 tbs

1. Heat the spinach with the butter and sprinkle with a couple of pinches of nutmeg.
2. Put into a small ovenproof dish and make a hollow in the middle.
3. Carefully break the egg into the hollow and sprinkle the cheese over it.
4. Bake in a preheated oven at 350°F/180°C/gas mark 4

for about 15 minutes or until the egg is set.
5. Serve with toasted special gluten-free bread.

Note to Cooks

Can also be served as a poached egg on top of cooked spinach, without the cheese.

BAKER'S OMELETTE

Serves 3–4

Metric/Imperial		American
1	small onion, peeled and chopped	1
1 tbs	sunflower oil	1 tbs
2	boiled potatoes, sliced	2
2	tomatoes	2
2	medium-sized mushrooms	2
1 heaped tbs	cooked peas or chopped cooked vegetables	1 heaped tbs
6	eggs	6
	sea salt and freshly ground black pepper	
1 tsp	freshly chopped parsley	1 tsp

1. Preheat oven to 450°F/220°C/gas mark 7 and out in a largish, shallow, ovenproof dish to warm on the top shelf.
2. Fry the onion in the oil for about 5 minutes.
3. Add the vegetables and gently heat through.
4. Transfer to the warmed dish.
5. Beat the eggs in a bowl and season.
6. Pour over the vegetables and bake on the top shelf for about 10 to 15 minutes until the eggs have set.
7. Sprinkle with the chopped parsley and serve hot with a side salad.

This recipe makes enough for 3 or 4 servings, so can be served to the whole family. A very quick and nourishing meal.

Gluten-Free

CHICKEN WITH ORANGE AND ROSEMARY

Serves 2

Metric/Imperial		American
2	chicken quarters, or breasts, skinned	2
3 pinches	salt	3 pinches
	freshly ground black pepper	
1 tbs	extra virgin olive oil (mild flavoured) or sunflower oil	1 tbs
1	onion, sliced	1
225ml/8 fl oz	orange juice	1 cup
½ tsp	dried rosemary	½ tsp
or		
1 tsp	fresh	1 tsp
1	small orange, grated rind of	1
2 slightly heaped tsp	gluten-free cornflour/ cornstarch, mixed to a paste with	2 slightly heaped tsp
2 tsp	cold water	2 tsp

1. Season the chicken all over with salt and pepper and rub in.
2. Heat the oil in an ovenproof casserole and fry the chicken pieces for about 7–8 minutes, turning them over to brown evenly.
3. Remove the chicken from the pan, add the onion and fry gently, stirring, for 5 minutes.
4. When the onion is soft, add the orange juice, rosemary and orange rind.

Main Meals

5. Put the chicken pieces back into the casserole and bring to the boil, then reduce the heat and simmer gently for about 30 minutes, until the chicken is tender. Transfer the chicken to a warmed serving dish and keep warm.
6. Stir the cornflour (cornstarch) paste into the liquid and bring to the boil. Cook, stirring for 2 minutes until it has thickened, then pour it over the chicken.
7. Serve hot with boiled rice and green beans or a green salad.

COTTAGE PIE

Serves 4

Metric/Imperial		*American*
2	medium-sized onions, sliced	2
2 tbs	vegetable oil	2½ tbs
½ kilo/1 lb	lean, minced beef	1 lb
1 tbs	ground brown rice	1 tbs
1 heaped tsp	tomato *purée*/paste	1 heaped tsp
3 tsp	gluten-free soy sauce	3 tsp
150ml/¼ pint	water	⅔ cup
	sea salt and freshly ground black pepper	
4 portions	hot, boiled potatoes	4 portions
25g/1oz	polyunsaturated soft margarine	2½ tbs
	a little water	
3 pinches	grated nutmeg	3 pinches

1. Preheat oven to 375°F/190°C/gas mark 5 and put a casserole in to warm.
2. Fry the onion in the oil for about 5 minutes.
3. Add the beef and fry very gently while stirring for another 5 minutes.
4. Sprinkle in the ground rice and add the tomato *purée* (paste) and soy sauce.
5. Stir well and add enough water to make a sloppy mixture.

6. Season and spoon into the warmed casserole. Put back into the oven to keep warm.
7. Mash the potatoes well, adding the margarine.
8. Pour in a little water and beat with a wooden spoon.
9. Add the nutmeg and season to taste. Give it a final stir and pile on top of the meat mixture, spreading it out evenly over the top with a fork.
10. Bake for about 30 minutes on the middle shelf, then serve hot with green vegetables and carrots.

Note to Cooks

Put into 4 suitable dishes and freeze until required. Defrost slowly and heat thoroughly before eating.

SPANISH OMELETTE

Serves 1

Metric/Imperial		American
1 tbs	vegetable oil	1 tbs
1	medium-sized boiled potato, cut into thick slices	1
1	small onion peeled and sliced finely	1
small piece	green or red pepper, cut into strips	small piece
2	medium-sized tomatoes, sliced	2
½	small clove garlic, peeled	½
2	eggs	2
1 tsp	cold water	1 tsp
	sea salt and freshly ground black pepper	

1. Put the oil into a heavy-based frying pan.
2. Heat the potato slices and the onion.
3. Fry, turning once, for about a minute on each side.
4. Add the strips of pepper and the tomatoes. Crush in the garlic and distribute it in the pan.
5. Beat the eggs lightly with the water and when you think the pan is hot enough, pour over the cooked mixture. Cook for a minute or two until the eggs have set.
6. Season to taste and loosen the omelette with a spatula. Serve immediately on a hot plate with a green side-salad.

Note to Cooks

A good quick meal that makes the minimum of washing-up! Some people prefer it without the pepper (green or red) as they find it rather indigestible.

PLAICE WITH CUCUMBER

Serves 1

Metric/Imperial		*American*
1	fillet of plaice	1
1 tbs	ground brown rice mixed with	1 tbs
2 pinches	sea salt	2 pinches
25g/1oz	polyunsaturated soft margarine	2½ tbs
3.5cm/1½in.	cucumber, peeled and cut into thick slices	1½ in.

1. Put a dinner plate to warm.
2. Wash the plaice fillet and coat with the rice.
3. Put the margarine into a frying pan, heat and use to fry the plaice, turning once. This should take about 4 minutes.
4. Take the pan off the heat and remove the fish with a spatula. Put on to the warmed plate and keep warm.
5. Add the lemon juice to the pan, stir and return to the heat.
6. Add the cucumber slices and quickly heat through. Arrange them on top of the fish.
7. Serve immediately with carrots, grilled tomatoes or any brightly coloured vegetables and plain boiled brown rice.

Note to Cooks

Seasoning is put on at the table.

FISH AND CHIP DINNER

Serves 1

Metric/Imperial		*American*
2	medium potatoes	2
2 tbs	extra virgin olive oil or sunflower oil	2 tbs
1	egg white	1
2 tsp	gluten-free cornflour (cornstarch) or ground rice	2 tsp
100–160g/4–6oz	portion of plain cod or haddock	4–6 ounce
2	tomatoes, halved	2
2 heaped tbs	frozen peas	2 heaped tbs

1. Preheat the oven to 450°F/230°C/gas mark 8.
2. Peel the potatoes and cut them into chips (French fries). Put them in a roasting tin (pan) with 2 teaspoons of the oil and turn them over by hand to coat them.
3. Roast on the top shelf of the oven for about 20–25 minutes.
4. After 15 minutes, beat the egg white with the cornflour (cornstarch) or ground rice and use to coat the fish. Arrange the tomato halves in a small ovenproof dish and put into the oven on the bottom shelf.
5. Put the peas on to cook in boiling water. Heat the remaining oil in a frying pan and fry the fish over a moderate heat for 5 minutes. Carefully turn it over and cook the other side.

Gluten-Free

6. Serve on a warm plate with the chips, tomatoes and peas.

Note to Cooks

Going to someone else's house for a meal can be a nightmare for the gluten-free dieter and the host or hostess who wants to help but doesn't understand the diet. Here is an easy main meal within the capabilities of any cook. You may need to take your own gluten-free cornflour (cornstarch) or some ground rice, just to make sure.

LAMB WITH HERBS

Serves 1

Metric/Imperial		American
1 or 2	lamb chops	1 or 2
1	clove garlic	1
	dried rosemary	
	sea salt and freshly	
	ground black pepper	

1. Trim the chops of fat and wash them under the tap. Dry and put into the grill pan on a grid.
2. Cut the clove of garlic in half and rub over the meat.
3. Sprinkle with a little rosemary and seasoning.
4. Grill for about 15 minutes, turning once.
5. Serve at once with boiled potatoes and hot green vegetables. Peas and carrots are especially good with this dish.

Note to Cooks

Unsuitable for pregnant women.

GRAVY

Many people believe that gravy can only be made with a stock/gravy cube or a packet mix. This is nonsense. The best gravy is made from the natural stock contained in meat juices, a little thickening such as maize flour (cornmeal) and the strainings from vegetables. A little soy sauce can be added for colouring and extra flavour.

1. Strain the fat off the meal off the meat juices from the grill or roasting pan.
2. Sprinkle in about 1–2 heaped teaspoonsful of maize flour (cornmeal) and rub it into the juices with a wooden spoon.
3. While you heat, gradually add the strainings from any vegetables you have cooked, and 1–2 teaspoonsful of gluten-free soy sauce.
4. Stir while it thickens and serve hot with the meat and vegetables. If it turns out lumpy, then strain before using.

Variation:

Use half a boiled and well mashed potato as a thickener instead of the maize flour (cornmeal).

Note to Cooks

It is important to strain off all the fat from the meat juices or the gravy will be far too greasy.

LIVER WITH ORANGE

Metric/Imperial		American
50g/2oz	lamb's liver	1 medium-sized piece
1 tbs	vegetable oil	1 tbs
½	peeled orange, cut into slices	½
2 tsp	gluten-free soy sauce	2 tsp
1 tbs	pure orange juice	1 tbs

1. Cut out any stringy pieces from the liver. Wash, dry and cut it into small pieces.
2. Heat the oil in a frying pan and put in the liver. Fry gently while turning to cook evenly for 5 minutes.
3. Add the orange slices, soy sauce and orange juice. Heat through gently.
4. Serve hot with green vegetables and either plain boiled brown rice or potatoes.

Variation:

If you prefer a thicker gravy, dip the liver pieces in maize flour (cornmeal) before frying. (Seasoning is added at the table.) Unsuitable for pregnant women.

COLD MEAT AND SALADS

Beef, lamb and pork slices cut off a cold joint roasted the day before make an easy meal with salad and jacket potatoes. Here are some salad suggestions. Instructions for the jacket potatoes on pages 24–5.

RED SALAD

Serves 4

The colour of this salad is simply amazing!

Metric/Imperial		American
75g/3oz	red pepper, cut into strips	½ cup
150g/6oz	red cabbage, shredded	1 cup
100g/4oz	carrot, grated	1 cup
100g/4oz	fresh tomato, chopped	1 cup
100g/4oz	raw beetroot, grated	1 cup

1. Wash and prepare the vegetables.
2. Cut the red pepper into strips.
3. Shred the red cabbage finely.
4. Grate the carrot.
5. Cut the tomato into small pieces.
6. Grate the beetroot coarsely.
7. Combine all the ingredients in a bowl and dress lightly before serving with an oil and vinegar dressing and a seasoning of sea salt and black pepper.

Variation

For a slightly sweet salad sprinkle a little raw cane sugar over the finished salad. (This is especially good with cold pork or ham.)

GREEN SALAD

There are several types of greens, other than lettuce, that can be used for a green salad. Any mixture of the following on a base of either lettuce or cabbage will make an excellent salad.

Watercress – washed very carefully. Discard tougher stems and any discoloured leaves. Tear into sprigs.

Cress or Mustard Greens – cut off as near to the roots as you can and rinse in a colander under the cold tap.

Cabbage – choose heart leaves that will not be too tough. Wash and trim coarse stalks away. Shred finely.

Spinach – use young, tender leaves. Cut our coarse stalks. Tear the leaves into small pieces.

Kale – use only tender leaves. Wash well and tear or cut into small pieces.

Brussels Sprouts – trim, wash and shred finely.

Lettuce – wash leaves well and pat dry with a clean tea-towel. Tear into pieces.

Sliced spring onions (scallions) or the ordinary type of onion (chopped or sliced into rings) can also be used in a green salad; cucumber and finely chopped fresh parsley also make useful garnishes. Serve with an oil and vinegar dressing, but first sprinkle the mixed salad with a few pinches of sugar, sea salt and freshly ground black pepper.

OIL AND VINEGAR DRESSING

Put 1 tablespoonful of wine or cider vinegar and 3 tablespoonsful (3½ US) extra virgin olive oil into a screw-top
jar. Shake well before using. (This dressing should be
used to moisten salads not to swamp them.)

STIR-FRY VEGETABLES

This is a quick method of partly cooking vegetables so
that they are just soft enough to eat. Use a large flat pan
with sloping sides. Prepare a mixed selection of vegetables, cutting them into small pieces or thin slices (root
vegetables). Always start with a sliced onion and a tablespoonful of sunflower oil. Stir while you fry this for 3
minutes. Now add the rest of the vegetables in order of
hardness, carrot first, cucumber and tomato last. As you
put them in, use the middle of the pan and keep turning
them over. Push the cooked vegetables to the side of the
pan and the raw ones into the middle. Add a sprinkling of
sea salt and a tablespoonful or two of water. Mix a little
gluten-free soy sauce with the juices and you have a
lovely gravy. What could be easier?

SAVOURY RICE

Serves 2

Metric/Imperial		American
1	medium-sized onion, peeled and chopped	1
1 tbs	sunflower oil or similar	1 tbs
½	green pepper, de-seeded and chopped	½
1	carrot, scrubbed and chopped	1
1	stalk of celery, washed and chopped	1
3	Brussels sprouts or	3
2	tender cabbage or spinach leaves, shredded after trimming	2
1 portion	cooked brown rice sea salt and freshly ground black pepper to taste squeeze of lemon juice (optional)	1 portion

1. Fry the onion gently in the oil for a few minutes.
2. Add the prepared vegetables and a little water to prevent sticking.
3. Cook with the lid on tightly for about 6 or 7 minutes.
4. Add the cooked rice and mix everything together. Cook until the rice has heated through.
5. Season and add the lemon juice, if liked.

Gluten-Free

6. Serve hot with fish or meat.

Variation

Other kinds of vegetables can be used according to season – green beans, peas, turnips, parsnips, broad beans (Windsor beans) etc. If you want to use tomato this is best served as a garnish as it is very soft when cooked and tends to make the dish too moist.

BASIC SAVOURY SAUCE MIX

Metric/Imperial		American
1 tbs	butter or margarine	1 slightly heaped tbs
15g/½oz	gluten-free cornflour (cornstarch)	1 tbs
¼ litre/½ pint	milk	1⅓ cups
	flavouring from following list	
	sea salt and freshly ground	
	black pepper	

1. Melt the margarine in a saucepan.
2. Blend the maize flour (cornmeal) and milk in a bowl, stirring out any lumps.
3. Pour this into the pan with the margarine and stir well.
4. Add the flavouring of your choice.
5. Heat through and simmer for about 3 minutes, stirring all the time while the mixture cooks.
6. Serve hot, immediately, on fresh vegetables or fish.

Note to Cooks

Make sure the cornflour (cornstarch) is gluten-free.

FLAVOURINGS

PARSLEY – add one or two level teaspoonsful freshly chopped parsley.
MUSHROOM – add 50g/2oz fried mushrooms, chopped

very finely.

ONION – add one small onion, fried in a little sunflower oil until soft. Chop the onion very finely before frying.

TOMATO – add one tablespoonful tomato *purée* (gluten-free). Stir in well.

CHEESE – add 25–50g/1–2 oz ¼–½ cup grated hard cheese or Parmesan cheese. Cook the sauce while stirring until all the cheese has melted.

Serve any of these savoury sauces poured over baked, poached or steamed fish. Serve with a green vegetable such as peas and potatoes or rice, plain boiled.

CAULIFLOWER CHEESE

Pour hot cheese sauce over plain boiled or steamed cauliflower. Sprinkle a little more cheese on top and brown under the grill for a few minutes. The cauliflower should be tender but not soft as this will spoil the dish. Serve with special gluten-free bread and butter or margarine.

LEEKS IN CHEESE SAUCE

Metric/Imperial		American
1 portion	prepared leeks (generous)	1 portion
1	hard boiled egg	1
	cheese sauce	
	grated cheese for topping	

1. Cook the leeks, cut into short lengths, in boiling salted water until tender.
2. Strain well and put into an ovenproof dish.
3. Peel the hard boiled egg. Slice and lay on top of the leeks.
4. Cover with cheese sauce.
5. Sprinkle with grated cheese and grill until bubbling and just beginning to brown.
6. Serve hot with special gluten-free bread and butter or margarine.

POTATO 'SPAGHETTI'

Serves 1

Metric/Imperial		American
2	medium potatoes, peeled	2
1 tsp	olive or sunflower oil for greasing pan	1 tsp

1. Preheat the oven to 425°F/220°C/gas mark 7.
2. Thinly slice the potatoes lengthways and then cut them into long matchsticks. Place in a greased baking tin (baking pan).
3. Bake on the top shelf of the oven for 10 minutes, until tender but not crisp.
4. Serve in a mound, covered with a gluten-free sauce such as the one opposite.

SAUCE FOR 'SPAGHETTI'

Serves 1

Metric/Imperial		American
¼	onion, finely chopped	¼
1 scant tbs	olive oil	1 scant tbs
1 slice	lean ham (without breadcrumbs), cut into small squares	1 slice
2	tomatoes, chopped	2
½ tsp	tomato *purée* (paste)	½ tsp
1	mushroom (chopped)	1
¼ tsp	dried basil or	¼ tsp
½ tsp	chopped fresh basil	½ tsp
	salt and freshly ground black pepper	
1 tbs	Parmesan cheese, finely grated	1 tbs

1. Fry the onion in the oil for 4 minutes. Add all the remaining ingredients except the cheese and cook, stirring, for another 5 minutes.
2. Spoon the sauce over the Potato 'Spaghetti' (see opposite) or boiled rice and sprinkle with the cheese. Serve hot with a green salad or lightly cooked spinach or broccoli.

BOLOGNESE SAUCE

4 generous servings

Metric/Imperial		American
1	medium-sized onion, peeled	1
1 tbs	sunflower oil	1 tbs
1	clove garlic, peeled	1
4	small mushrooms, chopped	4
100g/4 oz	lean, minced(ground) beef	1 cup
½	small green pepper, de-seeded and chopped	½
4	medium-sized tomatoes, sliced	4
1 tbs	gluten-free soy sauce	1½ tbs
	sea salt and freshly ground black pepper	

1. Chop the onion and fry in the oil until transparent.
2. Add the minced (ground) beef and fry lightly, turning it over with a spatula until cooked.
3. Put in the garlic (crushed), mushrooms, peppers and tomatoes.
4. Mix and season with the soy sauce and salt and pepper.
5. Heat through and cook for about 10 minutes while you stir.
6. Serve hot on boiled rice or potatoes or potato spaghetti.

This can be re-heated the following day. Store overnight in the fridge, in a sealed container.

Gluten-Free

BAKED FISH

Metric/Imperial		American
1	portion cod, haddock or salmon fillet	1
	sea salt and freshly ground black pepper to taste	
½	lemon, juice of	½
1	orange, rind of	1
	small knob of butter	

1. Preheat oven to 375°F/190°C/gas mark 5.
2. Put the fish in a shallow ovenproof dish and season.
3. Pour the juice over the fish and sprinkle with the rind.
4. Dot with butter and bake uncovered for about 15 minutes near the top of the oven.
5. Serve immediately with stir-fry vegetable or savoury rice (page 90–91). Garnish with a sprinkling of parsley and a slice of lemon.

Note to Cooks

Salmon cooked this way is especially good with plain boiled new potatoes and broccoli florets. Garnish with lemon and parsley.

9

Puddings

FRUIT ON BREAD

Metric/Imperial		American
1 portion	stewed, sweetened fruit such as plums	1 portion
2 slices	special gluten-free bread sunflower oil for frying sugar for sprinkling	2 slices

1. Heat the fruit and keep warm.
2. Fry the bread in shallow, hot oil on one side only. Put on to a warmed plate and top with fruit.
3. Sprinkle with sugar and serve.

Variation

Any fruit from the plum family will do – damsons, green-gages etc. (This is a very simple dish but really delicious. Other fruits such as apples are not half as good.)

PEARS IN WINE

Metric/Imperial		American
1	stewing pear	1
1 glass	red wine	1 glass
4 good pinches	cinnamon	4 good pinches
	sugar to taste	

1. Peel and quarter the pear and place it in a small saucepan.
2. Pour the wine over the pear and cook over a gentle heat until the pear is soft.
3. Sprinkle in the cinnamon and sugar to taste.
4. Serve warm or cold.

Note to Cooks

If the liquid reduces too much while the pear is cooking, then top up with water. (This can also be cooked in the oven in a small casserole.)

CRUNCHY DATE TART

Metric/Imperial		American
Pastry:		
50g/2oz	polyunsaturated soft margarine	¼ cup
100g/4oz	ground brown rice	½ cup
75g/3oz	finely grated apple	1 small
Filling:		
100g/4oz	chopped cooking dates (or stoned eating dates)	⅔ cup
Approx. 200ml/⅓ pint	water	Approx. ¾ cup
40g/1½ oz	chopped nuts sprinkling of sesame seeds	¾ cup

1. Preheat oven to 425°F/220°C/gas mark 7.
2. Put the dates into a small saucepan with the water and cook until they form a stiff paste. Leave to cool.
3. Use a fork to blend the pastry ingredients. Knead into one ball of dough.
4. Grease a pie plate and line it with the dough by pressing out evenly with the fingers.
5. Raise a slight edge all the way round.
6. Spread the date mixture over the pastry.
7. Sprinkle with the nuts and seeds, pressing them in slightly.
8. Bake on the top shelf for about 20–25 minutes.

ORANGE CARAMEL

Metric/Imperial		American
1	large orange	1
1 heaped tsp	sugar	1 heaped tsp
1 tbs	water	1 tbs

1. Pare off half the orange rind as thinly as you can and cut into strips.
2. Cut off the remaining rind and the white, bitter pith.
3. Slice the orange and place it in a serving dish.
4. Put the strips of rind into a small saucepan and sprinkle with the sugar. Add the water.
5. Heat while you stir until the sugar has melted.
6. Continue heating and stirring until you have a bubbly golden brown caramel. Pour this quickly over the orange.
7. Allow to cool, then chill in the fridge. Serve cold.

APRICOT TART WITH ALMONDS

A refreshing pudding that can be served all year round,
hot or cold.

Metric/Imperial		*American*
Pastry:		
50g/2oz	polyunsaturated soft margarine	¼ cup
100g/4oz	ground brown rice	½ cup
75g/3oz	apple, grated	1 small
Filling:		
150g/6oz	dried apricots	1 cup
2 heaped tsp	sugar	2 heaped tsp
¼ litre/½ pint	water, cold	1⅓ cups
2 tsp	fresh lemon juice	2 tsp
25g/1oz	almonds, shelled and chopped	¼ cup

1. Preheat oven to 425°F/220°C/gas mark 7.
2. Pick over and wash the apricots before chopping them into small pieces.
3. Put into a saucepan with the sugar water and lemon juice. Bring to the boil and simmer until all the water has been absorbed.
4. Use a fork to blend the margarine, ground rice and apple. Knead until one ball of dough is formed.
5. Grease an enamel pie plate and put the dough in the centre. Flatten with the palm and fingers until it has

Gluten-Free

spread evenly over the plate. Raise a slight edge all the way round with the fingers.

6. Spread the filling evenly over the pastry and sprinkle with the almonds.

7. Bake for 20 to 25 minutes on the top shelf and serve hot or cold in slices.

FRUIT TART

Metric/Imperial		American
50g/2oz	polyunsaturated soft margarine	¼ cup
100g/4oz	ground brown rice	½ cup
75g/3oz	apple, finely grated	1 small
4 portions	stewing fruit	4 portions
200ml/⅓ pint or less	water	¾ cup or less
	sugar to taste	

1. Preheat oven at 425°F/220°C/gas mark 7.
2. Use a fork to blend the margarine, ground rice and grated apple. Knead in the bowl until it forms one ball of dough.
3. Grease an enamel pie plate and put the dough in the centre. Flatten with the palm of the hand and press out to cover the plate evenly. Raise an edge all the way round with the fingers.
4. Bake on the top shelf for about 20 minutes.
5. Prepare the fruit and stew it in a little water. Sweeten to taste.
6. When the base has baked take it out of the oven and spread with the stewed fruit. Serve hot or cold, cut in wedges.

Note to Cooks

Blackberry and apple, plums, damsons etc. are particularly suitable for this recipe.

Variations

Make the pastry base but bake for only 15 minutes. Take out of the oven and cover with a thin layer of raw sugar apricot jam (jelly). Cover this with overlapping thin slices of apple. Sprinkle with sugar and put back in the oven for another 10 minutes. Serve as Apple Tart.

Make the pastry base and bake for the full time. Spread with raw sugar jam when it comes out of the oven. Serve warm or cold as Jam Tart.

Make the pastry base and bake for only 15 minutes. Take out of the oven and spread with treacle. Sprinkle with special wheat-free breadcrumbs and put back in the oven for another 10 minutes. Serve hot or cold as Treacle Tart.

APPLE AMBER

Serves 4

This useful sweet can be eaten straight from the oven or cold from the fridge. Serve to the whole family or to guests if you are entertaining. Alternatively, halve the recipe and serve to the gluten-free dieter, hot one day and cold the next.

Metric/Imperial		American
500g/1 lb	cooking apples, peeled, cored and chopped	1 pound
small knob	butter	small pat
	brown sugar to taste	
1	lemon, grated rind and juice	1
2	egg whites	2
75g/3oz	caster (superfine) sugar	⅓ cup

1. Preheat the oven to 250°F/130°C/gas mark 1/2).
2. Put the apples in a pan with the butter and 1 table-spoon of water to prevent sticking. Cook gently until tender, then sweeten to taste with brown sugar.
3. Stir in the lemon rind and juice and then cook for another 5 minutes, stirring constantly. Transfer to an ovenproof pie dish.
4. Whisk the egg whites until very stiff. Fold in about 50g/2oz of the caster (superfine) sugar and pile lightly on top of the apple mixture. Sprinkle the remaining sugar over the meringue and bake for 30–40 minutes, until crisp on top.

CAROB PUDDING

Serves 2

Metric/Imperial		*American*
¼ litre/½ pint	water, cold	1⅛ cups
2 slightly heaped tbs	ground brown rice	2½ slightly heaped tbs
2 tsp	vegetable oil	2 tsp
3 heaped tsp	sugar	3 heaped tsp
15g/½oz	ground almonds	1 tbs
1 heaped tsp	carob powder	1 heaped tsp

1. Put the water and ground rice into a saucepan. Mix until smooth.
2. Add the oil and sugar and heat to boiling point. Cook while stirring for about 3 or 4 minutes, or until the pudding thickens.
3. Mix in the ground almonds and carob powder.
4. Serve hot or cold in 2 individual glasses.

Variation

Sprinkle with flaked almonds before serving.

Note to Cooks

If you do not have carob powder in the cupboard, use a gluten-free brand of cocoa instead.

FRUIT AND NUT CRUMBLE

Serves 2

Metric/Imperial		*American*
2 portions	sweetened, stewed fruit – any kind in season	2 portions
1 tbs	sunflower oil or similar	1 tbs
15g/½oz	ground almonds	1 tbs
100g/4oz	ground rice	½ cup
3 tsp	sugar	3 tsp

1. Preheat oven to 425°F/220°C/gas mark 7.
2. Put the stewed fruit into a small ovenproof dish and flatten the top evenly.
3. Put all the other ingredients into a mixing bowl and rub in with the fingers until the mixture resembles very fine breadcrumbs.
4. Spoon the crumble evenly over the stewed fruit, covering it all over. Make a hole in the centre to let out the steam.
5. Bake for about 10 to 12 minutes, until golden brown.
6. Serve hot or cold.

Gluten-Free

BAKED BANANAS

Serves 4

A simple but delicious pudding.

Metric/Imperial		American
4	bananas, peeled and cut in half lengthways	4
75g/3oz	sugar	½ cup
2	small oranges, juice of	2
25g/1oz	butter (optional)	2½ tbs

1. Preheat oven to 350°F/180°C/gas mark 4.
2. Put the halved bananas in an ovenproof dish.
3. Sprinkle with the sugar and pour the orange juice over the fruit.
4. Dot with the margarine.
5. Bake for about 15 minutes on the top shelf.
6. Serve hot on warmed plates.

CRÈME CARAMEL

Serves 3

This is a useful sweet as it can be made in advance and served from the fridge. Take care not to let the caramel darken too much.

Metric/Imperial		American
300ml/½ pint	milk	1¼ cups
40g/1½ oz	sugar	3 tbs
1	egg	1
1	egg yolk	1
few drops	vanilla flavouring	few drops

Caramel		
50g/2oz	sugar	¼ cup
2½ tbs	water	2½ tbs

1. Preheat the oven to 325°F/160°C/gas mark 3.
2. Put the ingredients for the caramel into a small heavy-based pan. Heat gently, stirring, until the sugar has dissolved.
3. Increase the heat and allow to come to the boil. Cook without stirring until the caramel turns a light nut-brown colour – about 3 minutes. Pour immediately into 3 ovenproof ramekins or a heatproof dish.
4. Put the milk and sugar in a pan and stir over a moderate heat until it comes to the boil. Remove from the heat and pour through a fine strainer.
5. Beat the egg and egg yolk together in a bowl until

thick and pale. Still beating, add the hot milk. Pour into a jug and stir in the vanilla flavouring.

6. Pour the milk and egg mixture into the prepared ramekins (or dish) through a fine strainer. Skim off any froth with a spoon.

7. Place the ramekins or dish in a deep baking tin (baking pan) and pour in enough boiling water to reach half way up the side of the ramekins or dish. Bake near the bottom of the oven for about 40 minutes or until set. Cool on a wire rack and then chill in the fridge.

8. When required, run a knife around the edge of the crème caramel. Out a serving plate upside-down on top, reverse the crème caramel and it will drop on to the plate.

Note to Cooks

Eat within 2 days.

THREE-FRUIT SALAD

Metric/Imperial		American
1	eating apple	1
	or kiwi fruit (peeled)	
1	orange, small	1
1	banana	1
1 small glass	unsweetened fruit juice	1 small
	(orange or pineapple)	glass
	sugar	

1. Prepare the fruits and cut into slices.
2. Pour the juice over the fruit and sprinkle with sugar to taste.

Variation

Other fruits in season can be used, e.g. pineapple, peach, strawberries, raspberries, nectarines, tangerines etc. Do not use more than three types of fruit. Clear honey can be used instead of sugar. (This is the easiest of puddings and can be eaten all the year round. Leave the skin on the apple for extra fibre and colour.)

BERRY CREAM

Serves 3

Metric/Imperial		American
¼ kilo/½ lb	raspberries or blackberries	2 cups
5 tbs	water	6 tbs
50g/2oz	sugar	⅓ cup
7g/¼oz	gelatine, dissolved in	1 tsp
2 tbs	cold water	2½ tbs
150ml/¼ pint	double (heavy) cream, lightly whipped	⅔ cup

1. Pick over the raspberries and wash them.
2. Put the fruit into the blender with the water and sugar and blend to a *purée* (sauce).
3. Put through a sieve to remove pips.
4. Gently heat the soaked gelatine until completely dissolved, then stir into the *purée* (sauce).
5. Leave until it is just beginning to set, then fold in the cream.
6. Turn the mixture into individual glass dishes to set and serve chilled.

Note to Cooks

Frozen raspberries, blackberries or summer fruits can be used.

APRICOT ICE CREAM

Serves 3

Metric/Imperial		*American*
150g/6oz	dried apricots	1 cup
1 tbs	fresh lemon juice	1 tbs
2	egg whites	2
75g/3oz	sugar	½ cup
150ml/¼ pint	double (heavy) cream, whipped	⅔ cup

1. Soak the apricots in water for about 2 hours.
2. Put the fruit into a small saucepan with enough water to cover and simmer gently for 20 minutes with the lid on.
3. Drain, saving 5–6 tablespoonsful of the liquid.
4. After cooling, put the cooked apricots, the reserved liquid and the lemon juice into the blender. Blend and cool completely.
5. Whisk the egg whites until stiff.
6. Gradually sprinkle in the sugar and whisk again.
7. Fold in the cream and apricot *purée* (sauce).
8. Turn the mixture into a freezer container. Cover, seal and freeze until the ice cream is solid.
9. Store in the freezer until required, and serve after transferring to the fridge for half an hour.

Note to Cooks

This is a useful recipe as it can be made all the year round.

Gluten-Free

BAKED APPLE

Metric/Imperial		American
1	cooking apple, large	1
	water	
	squeeze of fresh lemon juice	
	sugar to taste	

1. Preheat oven to 350°F/180°C/gas mark 4.
2. Wash the apple and, leaving it whole, cut a line around the middle. This will allow the flesh to expand during baking.
3. Cut out the core with an apple corer and discard.
4. Put the apple into an ovenproof dish and pour in about 150ml/¼ pint/⅔ cup of water.
5. Squeeze the lemon juice over the apple and sprinkle with sugar.
6. Bake for about 30 minutes on the top shelf.
7. Serve hot or cold.

Note to Cooks

For variations, stuff the apple cavity with sultanas, raspberries or blackberries.

BLACKCURRANT DESSERT

Metric/Imperial		American
1 slightly heaped tbs	ground rice	1 slightly heaped tbs
150ml/¼ pint	blackcurrants, stewed	⅔ cup
	sugar to taste	
1 tsp	sunflower oil	1 tsp

1. Put all ingredients into a small saucepan and mix until smooth.
2. Heat to boiling point and cook, while stirring, for 2 minutes or until thick.
3. Leave to grow cold. Serve chilled from the fridge.

ALMOND APPLE PUDDING

3 generous servings

Serve this to the whole family to prove to them how good gluten-free food can be. Double the recipe to make 6–7 servings.

Metric/Imperial		American
Base		
75g/3oz	brown sugar	⅓ cup
125ml/4 fl oz	water	½ cup
4	medium cooking apples, peeled, cored and cut into 8 wedges	4
Topping:		
40g/1½oz	butter	3 tbs
50g/2oz	caster (superfine) sugar	¼ cup
50g/2oz	ground almonds	½ cup
1	small lemon, juice and finely grated rind	1
1	egg, separated	1

1. Preheat the oven to 325°F/160°C/gas mark 3.
2. Put the brown sugar and water in a large saucepan and stir over a high heat until dissolved. Reduce the heat when it boils and continue to cook, without stirring, for about 4 minutes to make a syrup.
3. Add the apples to the pan, cover and cook gently for about 6–8 minutes, until tender.

4. Grease a sandwich tin (cake pan) large enough to hold the apples in one layer.

5. Beat the butter and caster (superfine) sugar until soft and light. Beat in the almonds, lemon juice and rind and egg yolk until well blended.

6. Whisk the egg white in a small bowl until it forms peaks. Use a metal spoon to fold it into the almond mixture.

7. Cover the base of the prepared tin (cake pan) with the apples, pouring over any remaining syrup. Spread with the topping and bake for about 20 minutes, until golden brown.

8. Cool in the tin (pan) for a few minutes, then serve with single (light) cream or on its own.

FRUIT BRULÉE

Serves 1

Metric/Imperial		American
1 portion	stewed fruit, sweetened to taste	1 portion
½ carton	natural yogurt	½ carton
3 tsp	sugar	3 tsp

1. Put the stewed fruit into an individual-sized oven-proof dish.
2. Pour or spoon the yogurt over the fruit.
3. Sprinkle the sugar over the top of the yogurt.
4. Place under a hot grill until the sugar melts. Watch it carefully so as not to let it burn.
5. Serve right away.

REAL FRUIT JELLY

Metric/Imperial		American
400ml/¾ pint	pure fruit juice	2 cups
15g/½oz	unflavoured gelatine crystals	1 tbs
	sugar to taste	

1. Put about one third of the fruit juice into a small saucepan and sprinkle in the gelatine crystals.
2. Stir well making sure there are no lumps.
3. Put over a very gentle heat and gradually bring to the boil, stirring all the time, to get out any lumps.
4. Add the rest of the fruit juice and stir well.
5. Put in the sugar to taste and stir until dissolved.
6. Pour into 3 or 4 individual glasses and leave to get cold.
7. Transfer to the fridge.
8. Serve cold, from the fridge, with a little single cream if desired.

For the fruit juice use any single juice or a combination of juices. Orange, liquidized strawberries, raspberries, cooked stoned prunes or dried apricots. Any left-over stewed fruit can also be used – blackberries, gooseberries, plums etc.

Note to Cooks

Avoid pineapple and kiwi fruit as these will not set.

TARTE DU JOUR

A colourful treat for elevenses, tea time or dessert, this tart can be served confidently to everyone, not just the gluten-free dieter.

Metric/Imperial		American
Pastry		
50g/2oz	gluten-free soft margarine	¼ cup
100g/4oz	ground rice	1 cup
75g/3oz	apple, finely grated	¾ cup
pinch	salt	pinch

Filling

Fresh fruit such as strawberries, raspberries or seedless grapes, stoned sweet cherries, peeled and sliced kiwi fruit or banana, or stoned and sliced peaches or nectarines.

2 tbs	apricot jam	2 tbs

1. Preheat the oven to 425°F/220°C/gas mark 7.
2. Put all the ingredients for the pastry into a bowl and blend with a fork until they form a dough.
3. Put the dough into the centre of an ovenproof plate or pie plate and gradually press it out with your fingers until the plate is evenly covered. Raise an edge all round by pinching between thumb and forefinger (flute it if you can).
4. Bake for 20–25 minutes until golden, then leave to cool on the plate.
5. When the base is completely cold, arrange the prepared fruit of your choice on top in concentric

circles – all one fruit or a variety.

6. Put the apricot jam in a small pan with 1 tablespoonful of water and heat gently, stirring. Brush over the fruit with a pastry brush and leave to set.

7. Serve the tart with single cream for a special treat or just on its own.

10

Tea Time

CHEESE AND APPLE MUFFINS

Makes 8

Metric/Imperial		American
50g/2oz	gluten-free polyunsaturated margarine	¼ cup
100g/4oz	ground rice	1 cup
75g/3oz	apple, finely grated	¾ cup
40g/1½oz	well-flavoured cheese, grated	⅓ cup
½ tsp	gluten-free mustard, such as genuine French mustard	½ tsp

1. Preheat the oven to 450°F/230°C/gas mark 8.
2. Mix the margarine and ground rice together with a fork. Stir in the apple, cheese and mustard until they are evenly distributed and one large ball of dough is formed.
3. Grease a baking (cookie) sheet and put 8 spoonsful of the dough on to it. Spread out into cookie shapes with a knife.

4. Bake at the top of the oven for about 20 minutes, until browned.
5. Leave to cool on the baking (cookie) sheet for 10 minutes, then transfer to a wire rack with a spatula to cool completely.

Note to Cooks

Eat within 2 days of baking. Pack in a lunchbox in place of bread rolls, or serve with soup or a meal.

DATE AND GINGER CAKE

Metric/Imperial		American
2 tbs	sunflower oil	2 tbs
50g/2oz	soft brown (molasses) sugar	¼ cup
1	egg, beaten	1
50g/2oz	ground rice	½ cup
25g/1oz	gluten-free cornflour (cornstarch)	¼ cup
25g/1oz	ground almonds	¼ cup
1 tsp	ground ginger	1 tsp
1	small eating apple, finely grated including skin	1
100g/4oz	dates, stoned and chopped	⅔ cup

1. Preheat the oven to 375°F/190°C/gas mark 5.
2. Put the oil, sugar, egg, ground rice and cornflour (cornstarch) into a bowl and beat until smooth.
3. Stir in the almonds, ginger, grated apple and dates. Mix well to distribute evenly.
4. Put the mixture into a greased and lined small loaf tin (loaf pan) and smooth the top with a knife.
5. Bake above the centre of the oven for about 45–50 minutes or until a skewer inserted in the centre comes out clean.
6. Cool in the tin (pan) for a few minutes, then turn out on to a wire rack to cool completely.
7. Wrap and store in an airtight container. Eat within 5 days. To freeze, wrap in individual slices.

ALMOND FRUIT PASTRIES

Metric/Imperial		American
50g/2oz	polyunsaturated soft margarine	¼ cup
100g/4oz	ground brown rice	½ cup
1	eating apple, large	1
50g/2oz	brown sugar	⅓ cup
25g/1oz	ground almonds	¼ cup
few drops	pure almond essence	few drops
	sliced almonds for decoration	

1. Preheat oven to 425°F/220°C/gas mark 7.
2. Blend margarine and ground rice using a fork.
3. Work in half the apple, grated, the sugar, ground almonds and flavouring. Knead until one ball of dough is formed.
4. Grease a baking sheet with margarine and put the dough in the middle. Flatten the dough out to a round shape by hand.
5. Cut the other half of the apple into thin slices and arrange these in the shape of a wheel, overlapping them slightly in the centre.
6. Sprinkle with a little more sugar and the sliced almonds.
7. Bake for 20 to 25 minutes until the pastry is cooked and the almonds toasted.
8. Allow to cool for a few minutes then serve, cut into wedges.

APPLE AND LEMON BUNS

Makes 6

Metric/Imperial		American
50g/2oz	gluten-free polyunsaturated soft margarine	¼ cup
50g/2oz	brown sugar	¼ cup
1	egg	1
100g/4oz	ground rice	1 cup
1	small apple, finely grated including skin	¾ cup
½	small lemon, finely grated rind	½

1. Preheat the oven to 375°F/190°C/gas mark 5.
2. Cream together the margarine and sugar. Add the egg and ground rice and beat until smooth.
3. Stir in the grated apple and lemon rind and spoon into a patty tin (muffin pan) lined with 6 paper cases.
4. Bake near the top of the oven for about 20 minutes, until golden, then cool on a wire rack. Eat within 2 days of baking.

Note to Cooks

Two of these buns served warm with gluten-free custard make a good pudding.

SPONGE BUNS

Metric/Imperial		American
50g/2oz	brown sugar	⅛ cup
50g/2oz	soft margarine	¼ cup
1	egg	1
70g/2½oz	*Trufree* No. 7 S. R. flour	¼ cup
few drops	vanilla flavouring	few drops

1. Preheat oven to 375°F/190°C/gas mark 5.
2. Line 6 patty tins with cake papers.
3. Put all ingredients into a bowl and beat to a cream.
4. Spoon into the cake papers and bake on the top shelf for 15 to 18 minutes.
5. Cool on a wire rack.

FRUIT SLICES

left-over gluten-free pastry
(from fruit tart etc.)
dried fruit
milk
sugar

1. Preheat oven to 425°F/220°C/gas mark 7.
2. Roll out the pastry and cut into 2 equal shapes.
3. Sprinkle one piece generously with dried fruit after brushing with milk.
4. Cover with the remaining piece of pastry and press the edges together.
5. Brush the top with milk and sprinkle with sugar.
6. Cut into fingers and place on baking sheet to bake for about 15 minutes. Serve freshly baked.

CURRANT CAKE

Metric/Imperial		American
50g/2oz	sugar	⅓ cup
50g/2oz	polyunsaturated soft margarine	¼ cup
2	eggs	2
100g/4oz	*Trufree* No. 7 S.R. flour	½ cup
100g/4oz	currants	⅔ cup

1. Preheat oven to 375°F/190°C/gas mark 5.
2. Grease and flour (with gluten-free flour) a small ½ kilo/1 lb loaf tin.
3. Put all ingredients into a bowl, except the currants and beat to a soft dropping consistency. Add a little milk if the mixture is too stiff.
4. Stir in the prepared fruit and put into the prepared tin.
5. Sprinkle the top with a little extra sugar (optional).
6. Bake for 30 minutes on the top shelf, then lower the heat slightly for another 30 minutes.
7. Leave to cool in the tin for a few minutes then turn out to cool completely on a wire rack.

SAND CAKES

Makes 6

Metric/Imperial		American
50g/2oz	gluten-free polyunsaturated soft margarine	¼ cup
25g/1oz	ground almonds or cashews	¼ cup
50g/2oz	sugar	¼ cup
1	egg	1
75g/3oz	ground rice	¾ cup
50g/2oz	sultanas (golden raisins), currants or raisins	⅓ cup

1. Preheat the oven to 400°F/200°C/gas mark 6.
2. Beat the margarine, ground nuts and sugar to a cream. Add the egg and ground rice and stir until combined.
3. Spoon into a patty tin (muffin pan) lined with 6 paper cases.
4. Bake above the centre of the oven for about 15 minutes, until golden. Cool on a wire rack and eat on the day of baking.

Note to Cooks

Although these look like ordinary buns they have a slightly gritty texture, hence the name. (Larger versions were popular in Victorian times when the texture was a novelty.) They tend to be rather dry, which means they do not freeze well. However, they are quick and easy to make, don't require a special flour and taste good.

FRUIT SCONES

Makes 8

Metric/Imperial		American
100g/4oz	*Trufree* No. 4 or 5 flour	1 cup
pinch	sea salt	pinch
1 tsp	bicarbonate of soda	1 tsp
1 tsp	cream of tartar	1 tsp
25g/1oz	polyunsaturated soft margarine	2½ tbs
25g/1oz	sugar	2½ tbs
25g/1oz	dried mixed fruit or just raisins or sultanas (golden seedless raisins)	2½ tbs
3 tbs	cold water	3½ tbs

1. Preheat the oven to 425°F/220°C/gas mark 7.
2. Put the flour, salt, bicarbonate of soda and cream of tartar into a bowl and mix thoroughly.
3. Add the margarine and rub it in with the fingers.
4. Stir in the sugar, dried fruit and water.
5. Mix, then kneed to a soft dough using a little more of the flour if you need to.
6. Divide into 8 portions, roll into balls, flatten and then shape into scones.
7. Put onto a greased baking sheet and bake on the top shelf of the oven for 15 to 20 minutes.
8. Eat freshly baked, split and spread with butter.

Note to Cooks

If you prefer, roll out the dough and cut into rounds with a cutter.

Gluten-Free

11

Celebration Food

PAVLOVA

4 Servings

Metric/Imperial		American
Meringue		
4	egg whites	4
2 pinches	salt	2 pinches
100g/4oz	soft brown (molasses) sugar	½ cup
1 tsp	gluten-free cornflour (cornstarch)	1 tsp
1 tsp	wine vinegar	1 tsp
Filling		
150ml/¼ pint	whipping cream (dairy)	⅔ cup
1 slightly heaped tsp	icing (confectioner's) sugar	1 slightly heaped tsp
few drops	vanilla flavouring	few drops
225–275g/ 8–10oz	sweet fresh fruit, prepared (see note overleaf)	8–10 ounces

1. Preheat the oven to 300°F/150°C/gas mark 2.
2. Whisk the egg whites with the salt until they start to look glassy. Whisk in half the sugar, a little at a time, whisking well after each addition.
3. Mix the remaining sugar and cornflour (cornstarch) together. Use a metal spoon to fold them into the egg whites. Sprinkle the vinegar over the mixture and fold in gently.
4. Lightly grease a piece of greaseproof (wax) paper and dust with a little gluten-free cornflour (cornstarch). Place on a baking (cookie) sheet.
5. Use a spatula to spread out the meringue in a circle on the greaseproof (wax) paper, building it up more around the edge.
6. Bake for 60–70 minutes, then open the oven door wide and leave the meringue inside for about 15 minutes. Remove to a draught-free place until completely cold.
7. Whip the cream until thick, adding icing (confectioner's) sugar to taste and the vanilla. Chill in the fridge until required.
8. When almost ready to serve, carefully peel the paper off the base of the meringue. Put the meringue on a serving plate and spread the cream in the middle.
9. Arrange the fresh fruit on the top and serve cut into wedges.

Note to Cooks

Suitable fruits are raspberries, strawberries, slices of kiwi fruit, mango, pineapple, peaches or nectarines, and stoned cherries. A mixture of three or four of these is attractive.

Have the meringue, cream and fruit ready prepared and assemble at the last minute. A truly spectacular dessert!

CHRISTMAS PUDDING

Metric/Imperial		American
15g/½oz	dried yeast granules	1 tbs
2 tbs	lukewarm water	2½ tbs
¼ litre/½ pint	orange juice	1⅛ cups
50g/2oz	brown sugar	⅓ cup
25g/1oz	soya flour	¼ cup
150g/6oz	ground brown rice	½ cup plus 2½ tbs
½ tsp	each gluten-free mixed spice, cinnamon and nutmeg	½ tsp
50g/2oz	polyunsaturated soft margarine, melted	¼ cup
1	small eating apple	1
1	small carrot	1
325g/11oz	dried mixed fruit	2 cups less 2½ tbs
1	lemon, grated rind of	1
1	orange, grated rind of	1

1. Put the yeast into a small basin with the lukewarm water and leave for 3 or 4 minutes to soften.
2. Stir to a cream and put the yeast into a large mixing bowl.
3. Heat the fruit juice until lukewarm, using a small saucepan.
4. Pour the juice over the dissolved yeast and mix well.
5. Add the sugar, soya flour, ground rice and spices and mix again.

6. Put in the margarine and grate in the apple and carrot. Beat until blended smoothly.

7. Add the fruit and rinds and mix well.

8. Grease a medium-sized pudding basin (1¼ litres/2½ pints, 1½ US quarts) and spoon the mixture into this. Tie on a double greaseproof paper lid and make a string handle.

9. Lower the basin onto a large saucepan about one-third full with boiling water.

10. Have either a grid or 3 metal spoons in the bottom to keep the base of the pudding off the bottom of the pan. Put the lid on and steam for at least 1½ hours. (Top up with *boiling* water if the level goes down.)

11. Put a warm serving plate on top of the pudding after removing the paper lid. Hold firmly together and turn the bowl upside-down. Shake the pudding out onto the plate and serve hot.

Note to Cooks

This is a rich golden pudding that will give 8 helpings. Apart from its colour, there is very little difference between this one and the traditionally made type. Serve it confidently to the whole family. Make on the day of eating.

If you prefer to use Easyblend/instant yeast, start at point 5 in the method adding 7g/¼oz (1 scant US tbs) and the warmed fruit juice.

STRAWBERRY GÂTEAU

Metric/Imperial		American
225g/8oz	caster (superfine) sugar	1 cup
225g/8oz	gluten-free soft polyunsaturated margarine	1 cup
4	eggs	4
225g/8oz	*Trufree* No. 7 S. R. flour	1 cup
50g/2oz	gluten-free cornflour (cornstarch)	¼ cup
few drops	vanilla flavouring strawberries, halved whipping cream (dairy)	few drops

1. Preheat the oven to 375°F/190°C/gas mark 5. Grease the edge of two 20cm/8 in sandwich tins (cake pans). Cut out 2 circles of greaseproof (wax) paper to fit the bottoms. Grease and place in the tins.

2. Put the sugar, margarine, eggs, flour, cornflour (cornstarch) and vanilla into a bowl and beat to a smooth, creamy consistency.

3. Spread evenly into the tins (cake pans), smoothing the top with a knife, and bake above the centre of the oven for about 20–25 minutes. (When done, the sponges should spring back if pressed lightly with a finger.)

4. Leave for a minute in the tins (pans), then turn out on to a wire rack to cool.

5. When cold, sandwich the cakes together with half the strawberries and whipped cream. Spread the top with the remaining cream and press the remaining strawberries into it.

Note to Cooks

Very showy for a celebration tea or as a dessert. Serve it with confidence as it tastes and looks the same as a cake made with ordinary flour. In winter, canned peach slices can be used instead of the strawberries.

BLACK FOREST GÂTEAU

Make as for Strawberry Gâteau but use only 200g/7oz (¾ cup) *Trufree* no. 7 flour and 25g/1oz (1¼ cup) gluten-free cocoa powder. Instead of strawberries, use stoned black cherries.

RICH FRUIT CAKE

Metric/Imperial		American
100g/4oz	gluten-free polyunsaturated soft margarine	½ cup
100g/4oz	soft brown (molasses) sugar	½ cup
2	eggs	2
100g/4oz	ground rice	1 cup
50g/2oz	gluten-free cornflour (cornstarch)	½ cup
50g/2oz	ground almonds	½ cup
2 tsp	(pure) ground cinnamon	2 tsp
1 tsp	gluten-free mixed spice	1 tsp
1	lemon, grated rind	1
few drops	almond flavouring	few drops
1	medium eating apple, finely grated including skin	1
350g/12oz	mixed dried fruit, washed	2 cups
75g/3oz	dried apricots, washed and chopped	½ cup

1. Preheat the oven to 350°F/180°C/gas mark 4. Grease and line a 18cm/7in round cake tin (cake pan).
2. Put the margarine, sugar, eggs and ground rice into a bowl and beat until smooth.
3. Add the cornflour (cornstarch), ground almonds, spices, lemon rind, almond flavouring and grated apple. Stir until well blended.
4. Stir in all the dried fruit and spoon into the prepared cake tin (cake pan).

5. Bake for about an hour on the middle shelf of the oven, until a skewer inserted into the cake comes out clean. Leave to cool in the tin (pan), then turn out.

Note to Cooks

This is not a cake for keeping more than week. Leftover cake can be sliced, individually wrapped and then frozen. (Allow several hours for defrosting). A slice warmed up and served with gluten-free custard makes a good pudding.

CELEBRATION CAKE

Metric/Imperial		American
225g/8oz	*Trufree* No. 7 S.R. flour	1 cups
3 pinches	salt	3 pinches
2 tsp	(pure) ground cinnamon	2 tsp
50g/2oz	ground almonds	½ cup
100g/4oz	brown sugar	½ cup
175g/6oz	gluten-free soft margarine	¾ cup
2 generous tsp	black treacle (molasses)	2 generous tsp
3	eggs	3
2 tbs	sherry	2 tbs
few drops	almond flavouring	few drops
50g/2oz	prunes, chopped	⅓ cup
100g/4oz	dried apricots, chopped	⅔ cup
350g/12oz	mixed dried fruit	2 cups
50g/2oz	dried mango or peaches, chopped	⅓ cup
1	lemon, grated rind	1
1	orange, grated rind	1

Topping (optional)

Redcurrant jelly/
marmalade
Marzipan (see page 147)
nuts, such as pecans,
walnuts, almonds and
cashews.

1. Preheat the oven to 325°F/160°F/gas mark 3. Line a 20–23cm/8–9in. round cake tin (cake pan) with greased greaseproof (wax) paper.
2. Mix together the flour, salt, cinnamon and ground almonds.
3. In a separate bowl, beat together the sugar, margarine and molasses until light and fluffy. Beat the eggs with the sherry and add to the margarine mixture alternately with the flour blend.
4. Stir in the almond flavouring, all the dried fruit and the lemon and orange rind. Mix well and spoon into the prepared tin (cake pan), then level the top with a knife.
5. Bake on the middle shelf of the oven for 1¼ hours, then lower the heat to 300°F/150°C/gas mark 2 and bake for another hour; cover the top with a piece of double greaseproof (wax) paper to stop it browning too much, if necessary. Test with a skewer. If it doesn't come out clean, bake for a few minutes longer.
6. Cool the cake in the tin (pan) overnight. Wrap in greaseproof (wax) paper and store in an airtight container for a week.
7. When ready to use, decorate the cake, if you like. Spread redcurrant jelly or marmalade over the surface to be covered. Cover the top with a thin layer of marzipan. Press nuts into it in neat circles to cover the whole top. Put a cake frill and bow around the sides and place on a cake board. Serve to everyone, not just the special dieter.

Note to Cooks

If you prefer a shiny finish for the top of the cake, boil a little sugar and water together to make a glaze. Paint on with a pastry brush and leave to set. If you want to make the cake well ahead of the celebration (not more than 3 weeks), store it, wrapped, in an airtight tin, as above but prick the top with a fork and drizzle in a little more sherry. This will ensure a moist cake. This cake is very high in calories and a slice per day is useful for people who want to maintain their weight when switching over from an ordinary diet to a gluten-free regime. It can also help to cheer them up if familiar treats are off the menu.

MARZIPAN

Store-bought marzipan is not usually gluten-free.

Metric/Imperial		American
225g/8oz	ground almonds	2 cups
100g/4oz	caster sugar	½ cup
100g/4oz	icing (confectioner's) sugar, plus extra for dusting	1¼ cups
½	egg, beaten	½
1 tsp	fresh lemon juice	1 tsp
few drops	almond essence	few drops

1. Put the ground almonds and sugars into a bowl and stir to combine.
2. Make a well in the centre and put in the lemon juice, almond favouring and egg. Knead into a ball.
3. Roll out the marzipan on a board dusted with icing sugar. Handle it as little as possible or it will be too sticky.

Note to Cooks

A perfectly acceptable celebration cake can be served *without* this very sweet topping. Marzipan is traditional but not essential. It is certainly not healthy.

SHERRY TRIFLE

1 serving

Use a *Trufree* sponge bun for the trifle base or make up
the Sand Cakes recipe (see page 133) but omit the fruit
and bake for about 12 minutes, until pale gold.

Metric/Imperial		American
1	*Trufree* sponge bun or Sand Cake (see above)	1
1 tbs	red jam	1 tbs
1 scant tbs	sherry	1 scant tbs
2 tbs	sliced canned peaches or apricots, with a little juice	2 tbs
about 4 tbs	gluten-free custard (use appropriate custard powder or gluten-free cornflour (cornstarch) and vanilla flavouring)	about 4 tbs
about 2 tbs	whipped cream (dairy)	about 2 tbs
1	glacé (candied) cherry, washed	1
a few	toasted almonds	a few

1. Slice the bun in two and sandwich together with the
   jam. Break into pieces, place in a glass dish and spoon
   over the sherry.
2. Arrange the peaches or apricots on top and spoon
   over a little juice.
3. Cover with the custard and leave to set.
4. Spread the whipped cream on top, sprinkle with the

almonds and put the cherry in the centre.

Note to Cooks

Make sure the cake base is nicely moistened with the jam, sherry and fruit juice.

JELLY TRIFLE

1 serving

Metric/Imperial		American
1	*Trufree* sponge bun or gluten-free trifle base (see Sherry Trifle)	1
4–5 tbs	hot, liquid fruit jelly Real Fruit jelly (on page 122)	4–5 tbs
2 tbs	sliced fresh or canned peaches or canned apricots	2 tbs

1. Break up the bun and put it in a glass dish.
2. Arrange the fruit on top of the sponge. Spoon over the jelly and leave to set.
3. Place in the fridge and serve within 48 hours, with cream if liked.

SAVOURY STRAWS

Metric/Imperial		American
25g/1oz	cold, boiled mashed potato	1 tbs
15g/½oz	polyunsaturated soft margarine	1 tbs
pinch	sea salt	pinch
50g/2oz	ground brown rice	¼ cup
1 heaped tsp	onion or shallot, very finely chopped	1 heaped tsp

1. Preheat oven to 425°F/220°C/gas mark 7.
2. Beat the potato to a cream with the margarine.
3. Gradually add the salt and ground rice and combine with a fork.
4. Put in the onion and mix well into one ball of dough. (If it too dry, add a little water.)
5. Press out by hand on a surface flavoured with ground rice.
6. Cut into fingers with a sharp knife and use a spatula to put them on a greased baking sheet.
7. Bake for about 8 to 10 minutes. (Do not overbake or they will be too crisp.)

12

Coping Generally

Packed Meals

Don't fall into the trap of putting up packed meals that are largely stodge. Try to imitate a meal eaten at home for balance. Soup can be taken in a thermos flask for instance. Salads can be packed in a screw-top jar with another small jar containing dressing to put on just before eating. Pack slices of cold meat between small sheets of greaseproof paper. Cheese can be grated and put into a small plastic container to be sprinkled over salad.

Instead of bread, slice cold cooked potatoes and put into a plastic box. Bananas, apples, pears and grapes make perfect snacks but don't forget dried apricots, raisins and sultanas (golden seedless raisins) as well as nuts of all kinds.

Try to make the basis of the packed meal a protein one – meat, fish, eggs, cheese or nuts. The energy part of the meal, bread and potatoes, should not be too much in evidence, nor should you pack too much sweet and sugary stuff. A slice of rich fruit cake is much better than chocolate bars or stodgy biscuits. If fruit becomes boring try fruit jelly which you can allow to set in a plastic container, or fresh fruit juice with an ice cube in a thermos flask for a cooling summer drink.

It isn't a bad idea to keep a note of just what you put into packed meals if you have to cope with this every day. You can then avoid too much repetition.

The secret really is always to try to make the special dieter's food enviable and this applies just as much to food you are sending out from home as the food you put on the table.

General List of Gluten-free Items

Bacon	Wine vinegar
Chopped peel and cherries	Fish (fresh, uncoated)
Cut mixed peel	Fruit (fresh)
Desiccated coconut	Dried fruit
Cornflakes	Canned fruit
Crisps (plain)	Meat (fresh)
Rice Krispies (UK)	Milk (fresh or dried)
Brown rice	Nuts (plain)
Ground brown rice	Pickled beetroot
Ground white rice	Pickled onions
Flaked rice	Red cabbage
Tapioca	Syrup
All kinds of cheeses (plain)	Black treacle
– not spreads	Honey (pure)
Cream (dairy)	Jam (jelly)
Fruit juices (unsweetened)	Lemon curd

Squashes	Marmalade
Chocolate (good makes)	Sugar (raw cane)
Cider	Other sugars
Wine	Vegetables (fresh)
Sherry	Natural yogurts
Brandy	Tea
Butter	Spices
Margarine (without wheatgerm oil)	Coffee (pure)
Oils	

Balancing Your Diet

The average Western diet has many faults – far too much fat, sugar and salt; too little of fresh vegetables, fruit and fibre-rich foods; too many over-processed junk foods etc. Try to avoid these dietary pitfalls and balance your diet in this way to rectify matters:

15% fats, oils (including cheese), nuts and seeds
20% meat, fish and eggs
45% fresh vegetables and fruit (including a green leafy vegetable daily)
20% special gluten-free bakery items, including bread

The basic food in a gluten-free diet is not balanced in the same way as a diet where gluten-containing foods are staples. Here are the basic food values in a gluten-free diet:

PROTEIN – meat, fish, eggs, nuts, dairy produce

FAT – cheese, cooking oils, fish and meat, nuts and seeds
CARBOHYDRATE – rice, potatoes, bananas, special bread and bakery items, sugar
FIBRE – soya bran, rice bran, root vegetables, dried fruits
VITAMINS AND MINERALS – fresh vegetables and fruit

A wide variety of fresh foods should give you all the nourishment you need for a healthy diet. However, food supplements (vitamins and minerals) can be taken if they are felt to be necessary. These should also be gluten-free (specially formulated) like the rest of the diet. (See shopping list for brands.)

Coping at Home

Some people can take the situation of having a special dieter in the family seemingly in their stride. Others are not able to cope quite as well. The dieter eats the wrong things and never seems to be really well. Perhaps the secret is to be really organized about it and if possible to get the full co-operation of the dieter.

Make sure your special store-cupboard is always stocked up. Teach the dieter to cook for him or herself if at all possible so that they will be able to cope with their own food in an emergency or just to give the usual cook a bit of a holiday.

If you can prepare things that the whole family can enjoy then so much the better – this saves preparing two kinds of food. Try to present the special food attractively and make it appetizing. Whatever you do, don't make the special dieter feel a burden. This can lead to

Coping Generally

emotional problems within the family unit.

Avoid a dull routine of cooking the same old recipes. There are several books available on gluten-free cooking now and this kind of exclusion diet isn't the dreary type it used to be, thank goodness. There are a variety of gluten-free diet foods available too. Try your local health store for these.

Don't forget, foods made from *wheat starch* are likely to contain gluten even though labelled 'gluten-free'.

Holidays

If going on a self-catering holiday you can take with you a variety of recipes made up, as far as possible, for cooking and baking during the holiday. For instance, you can make up a few of the bread mixes and take the yeast with you to bake as you need them. (Add the oil and water just before baking.) A rich fruit cake is a good standby and will keep a week at least. Biscuits can be made too and kept in an air-tight tin. Crumble topping can be made up and kept in the refrigerator (if there is one) and used as required.

If the holiday is not self-catering then you will have to take some of the special foods you know you won't be able to obtain. Again, a rich fruit cake is a good standby, also biscuits.

If possible, notify the catering manager or equivalent of the place where you plan to stay that you have someone in your party who is on a special diet. This can avoid misunderstandings with the serving staff who can take offence at someone whom they think is just plain finnicky and a nuisance. Very often it comes as a pleasant surprise that staff will take no end of trouble to make sure the special diet is accommodated. However, do not take this for granted and have some standby items just in case. **As a general rule, catering staff, however well qualified, have no knowledge of catering for a special diet.**

One golden rule – never go on holiday without your diet food list; and remember, hundreds of thousands of people cope daily with a special diet so you are not alone. Don't think of it as a terrible problem, just get yourself organized and take it in your stride.

13

Shopping

General Items

(Available at supermarkets or grocery stores)
Spices
Cooking oils
Instant yeast/easy blend yeast
Fruit juices
Wine or cider vinegar

Specialized Items

(Probably available at health stores, delicatessens or large chemists/drugstores)
Soya flour
Potato flour (farina)
Rice bran
Maize flour (cornmeal)

Very Specialized Items

(The *Cantassium Co.* has a mail order service, including export, for people on special diets)

Pectin (dried)

Special baking powder (gluten-free)

Maize flour (cornmeal)

Trufree vitamins and minerals

Trufree (gluten-free) flours

Trufree flours are specially formulated for the gluten-free dieter in the UK. They are made in carefully controlled conditions to be 100 per cent gluten free and are available from large chemists and some healthfood stores or by mail order in the UK and overseas. Write for details and sample if available, to Trufree Dept GFC, Cantassium Co., 225 Putney Bridge Road, London SW15 2PY (England). Enclose a piece of paper with your name and address in block capitals to avoid delay.

Special Baking Powder

Commercial baking powders are designed to work with gluten, and gluten containing grains are often used in their manufacture. In a gluten-free diet special baking powder is required. If you prefer to make your own here is a recipe:

Metric/Imperial		*American*
7g/¼oz	potassium bicarbonate	2 tsp
115g/4¼oz	potato flour (farina)	¾ cup

Mix these two ingredients together and store in a screw-top jar. Use as required. Try the chemists or drugstore for the first ingredient.

Pepper

A word of warning about the use of pepper. It is common practice in commercial catering to add wheat flour to ground white pepper to 'stretch' this expensive commodity. It is therefore a good practice to use only freshly ground black pepper when you are eating out.

Margarine

Some 'fancy' margarines have wheatgerm oil added. Check your labels as this is not gluten-free. (Butter is gluten-free.)

Soy Sauce

Most soy sauces are made from soy beans and wheat so are not gluten free. Look for Tamari type soy sauce which is made from soy beans and rice. This will be gluten free. Your local health store is the most likely place to find it. Check the label carefully before buying.

Index

Recipes for Health: Wheat, Milk & Egg-Free

Over 100 recipes which avoid these common allergens

RITA GREER

Are you allergic to milk, eggs or wheat, or do you cook for someone who is?

Wheat, milk and eggs are probably the three most common allergy-causing agents. As they play such an important part in the structure of our diet, a food regime which excludes them needs to be carefully balanced to be fully nutritious. This book is essential reading offering practical advice and over 100 delicious recipes which are easy to prepare and can be enjoyed by the whole family.

Rita Greer is a specialist in cooking and catering for people with special diets. She is the author of a number of successful special diet cookbooks.

Of further interest

Natural Therapies

The complete A–Z of complementary health

EDITED BY MARGOT MCCARTHY

Complementary or alternative therapies have become mainstream, but with so many to choose from, from acupressure to zone therapy, how do you decide which one is right for you?

This book, written by a team of qualified practitioners and edited by the proprietor of the well respected Neal's Yard Therapy Rooms in Covent Garden, London, is a complete introductory guide to alternative therapies, remedies, technique and treatments. Each entry includes:

- A brief history of the therapy
- A description of how it works
- The philosophy behind it
- How it interacts with other therapies
- What type of ailment it is particularly effective for.

Also included are easy reference charts; an overview of natural therapies and conventional medicine; an introduction to the body's systems; and a guide to what to expect from the therapist, what to ask for and what to check up on.

If you have ever considered visiting an alternative practitioner but are not sure exactly what might be involved, this guide is an indispensable starting point. If you are already visiting a practitioner but want to be better informed, this book will be invaluable.

Gluten-Free

Healing Through Nutrition

The natural approach to treating illness with diet and nutrients

DR MELVYN R WERBACH

This indispensable reference book provides the nutritional roots and cures for fifty common illnesses, from the common cold to cancer. Written by the world's authority on the relationship between nutrition and illness, Dr Melvyn Werbach's approach makes it easy to learn what you can do to influence your health via the nutrients that you feed your body.

In this highly accessible A–Z of nutritional health, a chapter is devoted to each of the fifty ailments, and includes:

- dietary factors affecting health and well-being
- a suggested healing diet for fifty common illnesses
- nutritional healing plans, with recommended dosages for vitamins, minerals and other essential nutrients
- explanation of vitamin supplements and how they can improve your health

There are also guidelines on how to plan the right healing diet for you and how to diagnose food sensitivities. With this groundbreaking guide you will be able to make informed decisions about the essential role of nutrients in your health and well-being.

Dr Melvyn R Werbach is a medical doctor, a member of the American College of Nutrition and assistant clinical professor at the UCLA School of Medicine. He is the author of the acclaimed *Nutritional Influences on Illness*, also from Thorsons, and *Third Line Medicine: Modern Treatment of Persistent Symptoms.*

Gluten-Free

Let's Eat Right To Keep Fit

'The Highest Authority in the Kitchen' *Time*

ADELLE DAVIS

Let's Eat Right to Keep Fit is a classic practical guide to nutritional health. Adelle Davis presents information concerning our bodies' vital nutritional processes which is both authoritative and fascinating. Her recommendations for a balanced diet are important for anybody interested in preventative medicine.

Adelle Davis discusses, in detail, over 40 nutrients needed by the body to build health, and lists the foods that supply them in the most concentrated form.

The author believes that since we cannot find adequate nutrition to sustain life from synthetic foods and vitamins, we need to find our real sustenance from good, wholesome food.

Adelle Davis is the author of several classic and revolutionary books on nutrition and health, including *Let's Get Well, Let's Stay Healthy*, and *Let's Have Healthy Children*. There are over 10 million Adelle Davis books in print.

Gluten-Free

Let's Get Well

ADELLE DAVIS

Let's Get Well explains how a well-chosen diet, which provides the most needed nutrients, can repair and rebuild a sick body. Packed full of information on every aspect of health and nutrition, it is an ideal reference book for the way we live today.

Adelle Davis explains the function of nutrition in diseases related to the blood system, the digestion, the liver, the kidneys and the nervous system. Illnesses covered include heart attacks, ulcers, diabetes, arthritis, gout and anaemia. Her clear explanations, with full medical references, will guide the way to better health.

Adelle Davis is one of the world's best-known advocates of health through good nutrition. She is the author of such classic books as *Let's Eat Right to Keep Fit* and *Let's Have Healthy Children*.

Gluten-Free

RECISPES FOR HEALTH:

WHEAT, MILK & EGG-FREE	0 7225 3197 4	£5.99	☐
NATURAL THERAPIES	0 7225 2830 2	£8.99	☐
HEALING THROUGH NUTRITION	0 7225 2941 4	£12.99	☐
LET'S EAT RIGHT TO KEEP FIT	0 7225 3203 2	£5.99	☐
LET'S GET WELL	0 7225 2701 2	£5.99	☐

All these books are available from your local bookseller or can be ordered direct from the publishers.

To order direct just tick the titles you want and fill in the form below:

Name: _____

Address: _____

_____

_____ Postcode: _____

Send to: Thorsons Mail Order, Dept 3, HarperCollins*Publishers*, Westerhill Road, Bishopbriggs, Glasgow G64 2QT.
Please enclose a cheque or postal order or your authority to debit your Visa/Access account –

Credit card no: _____

Expiry date: _____

Signature: _____

– to the value of the cover price plus:
UK & BFPO: Add £1.00 for the first book and 25p for each additional book ordered.
Overseas orders including Eire: Please add £2.95 service charge. Books will be sent by surface mail but quotes for airmail despatches will be given on request.

24 HOUR TELEPHONE ORDERING SERVICE FOR ACCESS/VISA CARDHOLDERS – TEL: 0141 772 2281.

Gluten-Free